Home Style

A room-by-room
guide to giving your home a new look

WARD LOCK

A WARD LOCK BOOK

First published in the UK 1996
by Ward Lock
Wellington House
125 Strand
London
WC2R 0BB

A Cassell Imprint

Copyright © Eaglemoss Publications Ltd 1996
Based on *Creative Ideas*

Distributed in the United States
by Sterling Publishing Co., Inc.
387 Park Avenue South, New York, NY 10016–8810

Produced by Brown Packaging Books Ltd,
255–257 Liverpool Road, London N1 1LX

A British Library Cataloguing in Publication Data block for this book may be obtained
from the British Library

ISBN: 0-7063-7564-5

Printed in Italy

Jacket photographs
Front: Dominic Blackmore/Robert Harding Picture Library (tl),
Steve Tanner/ Eaglemoss Publications (tr), Martin Chaffer/Eaglemoss Publications (bl, br)
Back: Martin Chaffer/Eaglemoss Publications (tl, tr, c), Adrian Taylor/Eaglemoss Publications (b)

Contents

Introduction

Choosing your own home decorating style has never been more enjoyable. This book gives you a room-by-room tour so you can see at a glance what goes with what.

There are a variety of looks that will suit different types of homes and different lifestyles, from city bachelor pads to family-filled rambling country houses.

Home Style *will show you how to combine colours and patterns, fabrics and paints so that each style can be tailor-made to suit you – choose from the elegant sophistication of a striking Black & White Sitting Room or let colour run riot in the Colour Theme Child's Room.*

The book gives easy to follow step-by-step instructions for making all the main items as well as all the clever little finishing touches in every room.

Classical Look Hall

Your hall is the ideal place to make a design statement — after all it is the first part of your house that everyone will see. The exciting project ideas here are perfect if you want to create a classical look.

In this room you can make:
- Elegant hall table cover
- Simple pleated paper lampshade
- Decorative embossed picture frame

Find out how to stain wood to give it new colour and depth.

For classical chic why not stitch an Assisi embroidery in black and white.

Keep things tidy with a letter rack and address book for your hall table.

YELLOW HALL

As your hall is the first glimpse that people have of your home, it's very important that it looks welcoming. The soft yellow used in this hall sets just the right warm note, and the practical hard-wearing black and white floor provides a smart contrast. Other warm colours would look good too – try apricot, pale pink or peach. Choose a pale shade for the walls and a stronger one for accessories, like the smart table cover.

To keep the colour scheme simple, black is the main accent colour. It's used on the floor and the woodwork, and it's repeated on the umbrella stand, the picture frames and in the smart silhouette pictures.

If you find that black is too harsh a colour, you could try a different accent colour, such as navy or dark green.

STAINING WOODWORK

The bannisters, dado rail and skirting boards in this hall have been coloured with wood stain for a warm dark glow. Wood stain brings out the beauty of wood, and can enhance or even change its natural colour: this woodwork was a pale pine colour, but now it resembles a rich hardwood.

Wood stains come in various colours and finishes. Traditional types need a final coat of varnish to provide a sheen, but other, more convenient finishes colour and seal in one go.

MATERIALS

Wood stain or all-in-one wood stain

Clear varnish (if using ordinary wood stain)

Lint-free cloth (if using ordinary wood stain)

Paintbrush

Fine sandpaper

Medium sandpaper

White spirit

Rubber gloves (optional)

Protective plastic sheeting or old newspapers

1 PREPARING THE SURFACE
Old wood: strip any existing paint or varnish with a proprietary stripper, then rub over the surface with sandpaper. Clean the wood with white spirit and leave it to dry.
New wood: make sure the surface is clean, dry and dust-free. Wipe over any resin knots with white spirit and leave it to dry.

2 APPLYING THE STAIN
Protect the surrounding surface with newspaper or protective sheeting. Apply the stain with a soft, lint-free cloth or with a brush, following the direction of the grain. Allow it to dry completely, then rub over it gently with fine sandpaper. Apply more stain until the colour is as deep as you want.

3 APPLYING VARNISH
The damp wood stain may have raised the grain, so lightly rub over the surface with fine sandpaper. Brush on a thin coat of clear varnish in the direction of the grain. Leave it to dry, then apply another coat.

USING ALL-IN-ONE STAIN

Apply the stain with a brush, working in the direction of the grain. Leave the first coat to dry, rub it down lightly with sandpaper then apply one or two more coats.

Classical Look Hall – Arranging pictures

Once you've decided on your hall's overall colour scheme, concentrate on the details to make an impressive focal point. Follow the steps to make plain frames quirky and original, and embroider an Assisi-work dove in cross stitch and backstitch.

▼ To create a stylish first impression, display your pictures in the hall in elegant frames, cleverly decorated with mouldings and embossed wallpaper.

DECORATING FRAMES

The ornate frames in this hall look very impressive, with their elaborate mouldings and antique-look gilded finishes. The simple instructions show you how to recreate these looks by embellishing plain shop-bought frames with wooden mouldings, embossed wall-paper borders, paints, and gilt wax.

MOULDED FRAME

For a classical look, decorate a picture frame with small wooden mouldings, paint it and then add gilt wax for an authentic-looking 'gilded' finish. You can buy the mouldings from super-stores and DIY shops. Gilt wax is sold by artists' suppliers.

MATERIALS

Plain picture frame

Wooden motifs

PVA wood adhesive

Black or brown paint or wood stain and varnish

Gilt wax

Small paintbrush

Soft cloth

2 COLOURING THE FRAMES
Paint the frame with gold or black paint and leave it to dry. Alternatively, for a bare wood frame, apply wood stain and varnish (see STAINING WOOD, page 6).

1 ADDING THE MOTIFS
Make sure that the frame is dry and grease-free. Glue the motifs to the frame with PVA wood adhesive, and leave them to set.

3 ADDING THE GILT WAX
Using your finger, smooth a very small quantity of gilt wax over the mouldings and edges of the frame to highlight the raised details. Buff the wax to a sheen with a soft cloth.

moulded frame

moulded frame

embossed frame

EMBOSSED FRAME

Imitate the look of ornately carved wood by covering a plain frame with an embossed wallpaper border. Paint it black or brown, then add a little gilt wax for a realistic antique finish.

MATERIALS

Wide, plain picture frame

Self-adhesive vinyl wallpaper border with a raised design

Dark brown or black emulsion paint

Paintbrush

Gilt wax

Ruler

Pencil

Scissors

Soft cloth

1 CUTTING THE BORDER TO FIT
Cut four lengths of the border a little longer than each frame edge. If necessary, trim these lengths to the same width as the frame.

2 MITRING THE CORNERS
Peel the backing paper off the wallpaper border and stick it on the frame, overlapping the strips at the corners. Draw a straight line from the inside corner to the outside edge of the frame. Cut along the line through both layers. Press the borders to stick them down firmly.

3 COLOURING THE BORDERS
Paint the frame with two coats of black or brown emulsion paint and leave it to dry. Finish with gilt wax to highlight the raised design (see MOULDED FRAME, step 3)

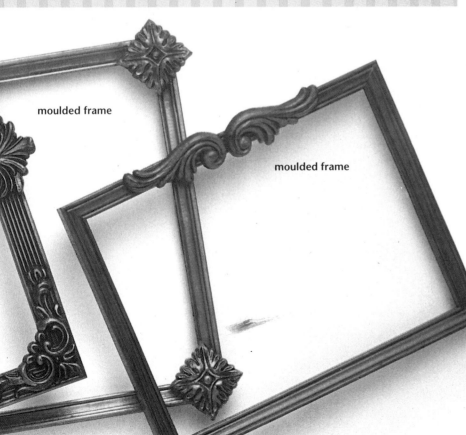

moulded frame

moulded frame

WIDE PICTURE FRAME

You can make a narrow frame wider by sticking timber round the edges. Cover the joins with an ornate painted and gilded wallpaper border.

MATERIALS

Picture frame

Timber, cut to the same thickness as the outside edge of the frame

Wooden moulding to edge the frame

Tenon saw

Mitre box

PVA wood adhesive

Self-adhesive vinyl wallpaper border with a raised design

Black or brown emulsion paint

Paintbrush

Gilt wax

Soft cloth

1 ADDING THE EXTENSIONS
Using the tenon saw, cut two pieces of timber to fit two opposite sides of the frame. Glue them in place. Cut two more pieces to fit the remaining sides, including the extensions created by the extra timber, and glue these in place. Leave the glue to dry.

2 ADDING THE EDGE MOULDINGS
Cut the edge moulding to fit all four sides of the frame, mitring the corners with the tenon saw and mitre box. Glue the edge moulding strips in place.

3 DECORATING WITH A BORDER
Cut the wallpaper border to fit the timber extensions, mitring the corners; paint it and then finish it with gilt wax (see EMBOSSED FRAME, steps 1-3).

POSY IN A BOX FRAME

Add extra interest to your display of pictures by including framed 3-D objects, like this pretty posy. You'll need a much deeper frame, called a box frame, to display it. Follow these instructions to convert an ordinary frame into a box frame for a posy or any other 3-D arrangement.

MATERIALS

Picture frame

Silk flower posy

12 x 45mm (½ x 1¾in) wood strip, twice the length plus twice the width of the frame

PVA wood adhesive

Clear adhesive

Gold spray paint

Black mounting board to line the box

Panel pins

Tenon saw

Narrow braid trim twice the length of the frame plus twice the width

Buttons with shanks to match the trim

Strong scissors

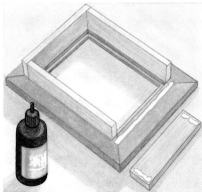

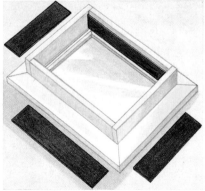

▲ The elegant box frame used to display this pretty silk flower posy is really an ordinary frame which has been converted, painted and then trimmed with braid and buttons.

3 TRIMMING THE FRAME
Cut the braid into four lengths to fit each side of the frame, and stick them in place with clear adhesive. Snip off the button shanks and stick the buttons over the joins in the braid.

1 MAKING THE BOX
Remove the backing board and glass from the frame. Cut two pieces of wood strip to fit two opposite sides of the opening at the back of the frame, and stick them in place with PVA wood glue. Cut two more pieces of wood strip to fit the remaining sides, overlapping the ends of the previously glued pieces. Stick these on and leave the glue to dry.

2 ASSEMBLING THE FRAME
Spray the frame all over with two coats of gold paint, following the manufacturer's instructions. Leave the paint to dry. Replace the glass. Cut two 4cm (1½in) wide strips of mounting board to fit inside two opposite sides of the box, and glue these in place with clear adhesive. Cut two more strips to fit the remaining two sides, and glue them in place.

4 FILLING THE BOX
Cut a piece of black mounting board the same size as the backing board. Glue the posy to the centre of the mounting board and leave it to set. Carefully place the mount face down over the back of the frame and place the backing board on top. Secure the backing with panel pins.

ASSISI WORK EMBROIDERY

Having a framed piece of your own handiwork in your hall will make an eye-catching conversation piece. This attractive black and white dove is a beautiful example of a traditional type of embroidery known as Assisi work. In this type of embroidery, the background of the design is filled in, while the motifs are left as an outline, creating an elegant silhouette effect. As in this striking dove picture, Assisi embroideries often have simple geometric borders. The stitching is always done in a dark colour on a white or cream fabric.

Stitch the embroidery in black to create a strong impression, and then frame it to match.

MATERIALS

15cm (6in) square of white Aida fabric with 18 threads to 2.5cm (1in)

Black stranded embroidery cotton

Embroidery needle

Embroidery hoop

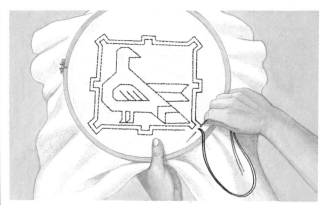

1 WORKING THE OUTLINES
Thread your needle with two strands of embroidery cotton. Using the chart as a guide, work the outlines in backstitch over two threads of fabric.

2 COMPLETING THE DESIGN
Fill in the shaded areas of the design with cross stitch over two threads. Press the embroidery on the wrong side and frame it to match the other pictures in your hall.

Classical Look Hall – Accessories

Smart accessories provide the final touches to your classical look hall. Create an elegant impression with a stylish black and white letter rack and notepad, and then emphasize your arrangement with candlestick lamps topped with pleated paper shades.

▼ Complete your classical look hall with these smart accessories. The letter rack and notepad are covered with fabric and topped with gilded mouldings.

LETTER RACK

Store your mail in a sturdy letter rack in smart black and white check. It's made from medium density fibreboard (MDF) which is inexpensive, easy to cut and widely available. Some suppliers will cut the MDF to size for you.

MATERIALS

25 x 80cm (10 x 31½in) rectangle of 9mm (⅜in) deep MDF

50cm (½yd) of 115cm (45in) wide gingham fabric

50cm (½yd) of 90cm (36in) wide lightweight fusible interfacing

15 x 25cm (6 x 10in) rectangle of dark felt

Moulded wooden motif

Black paint

Gilt wax (Treasure Gold)

PVA wood adhesive

Rubber-solution glue

Tenon saw to cut the MDF

CUTTING LIST

Fuse the interfacing to the back of the fabric, then cut out the following:
From interfaced fabric
● Two 23 x 18cm (9 x 7in) rectangles
● One 110 x 28cm (43½ x 11in) strip
From MDF
● One 15 x 25cm (6 x 10in) rectangle for the base
● One 10 x 25cm (4 x 10in) rectangle for the front upright
● One 15 x 25cm (6 x 10in) rectangle for the middle upright
● One 20 x 25cm (8 x 10in) rectangle for the back upright
● Two 6 x 25cm (2¼ x 10in) rectangles for the dividers

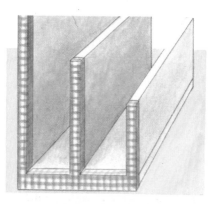

▲ This useful letter rack is made from MDF, so it's hard-wearing. It's covered in black and white checked fabric, but if you've chosen a different colour as your accent, then use a covering fabric in that colour.

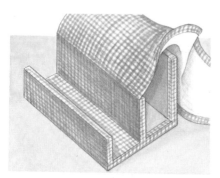

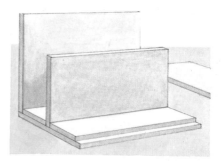

1 GLUING THE UPRIGHTS
Using PVA glue, stick the middle upright to the centre of the base, then glue a divider on each side. Stick the front and back uprights to each end of the base piece. Leave the glue to dry.

2 COVERING THE EDGES
Using rubber solution glue, stick a small rectangle of fabric to each end of the rack. Trim the fabric to 1.5cm (⅝in) beyond the edges, and clip diagonally into the corners. Press the fabric round the edges. Leave it to dry.

3 COVERING THE RACK
Fold under 1.5cm (⅝in) on both long edges and one short edge of the large fabric strip, and stick them down. Glue the short folded edge to the bottom of the front upright, then glue the fabric over to the back. Glue the felt to the base.

4 ADDING THE WOODEN MOTIF
Paint the wooden motif black and leave it to dry. Using your fingertip, rub the gilt wax over the raised details. Buff the wax to a shine with a soft cloth. Use PVA adhesive to stick the motif centrally to the front of the rack.

NOTEPAD

This cover is designed to fit a standard A6 notepad; these pads are widely available from stationers.

MATERIALS

A6 notepad

Two 16 x 12cm (6¼ x 4¾in) rectangles of mounting board

32 x 11cm (12½ x 4¼in) rectangle of black card

36.5 x 15cm (14½ x 6in) rectangle of gingham fabric

36.5 x 15cm (14½ x 6in) rectangle of lightweight fusible interfacing

30cm (⅓yd) of 9mm (⅜in) wide black elastic for the holding straps

Clear adhesive

Rubber solution glue

Moulded wooden motif

Black paint

Gilt wax (Treasure Gold)

Ruler and craft knife

2 MAKING A CARD LINING
Lay the card right side down and use the ruler and craft knife to score a foldline 15.5cm (6⅛in) from each short edge to form a 1cm (⅜in) wide central spine.

Cut two 14cm (5½in) lengths of elastic. Lay one strip 2.5cm (1in) from one short edge and the other strip 12cm (4¾in) from the edge. Use clear adhesive to secure the ends of the elastic to the back of the board.

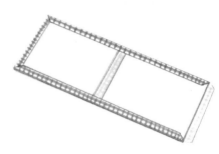

1 COVERING THE CARD
Fuse the interfacing to the wrong side of the fabric. Leaving a 1.5cm (⅝in) gap across the centre, glue the two small board rectangles to the fabric. Fold the edges of the fabric over the board, cutting it at the corners to make neat mitres. Glue these down.

3 FINISHING THE COVER
Using clear adhesive, stick the card centrally to the inside of the cover. Paint the wooden moulding and gild it, as for the LETTER RACK, step 4. Glue the moulding to the front of the cover, then insert the notepad.

LAMPSHADE

This stylish Empire lampshade is easy to make – it's simply made from pleated wallpaper. For an extra stylish look you can use left-over wallpaper from your hall, so you can match up your decorations perfectly.

MATERIALS

14cm (5½in) wide, 11cm (4¼in) deep Empire lampshade frame with a bulb clip fitting

73 x 15cm (28¾ x 6in) rectangle of wallpaper

80cm (⅞yd) of narrow cord elastic

1m (1⅛yd) of 6mm (¼in) wide ribbon

Clear craft adhesive

Ruler and pencil

Large tapestry needle

Hole punch

1 MARKING THE PLEATS
Lay the wallpaper down, wrong side up. Starting at one short edge, mark 1.5cm (⅝in) pleats along each long edge with the pencil. Using the ruler and the needle, score lines between opposite marks. The last score line will be 1cm (⅜in) from the cut edge.

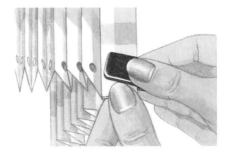

2 MAKING THE SHADE

Fold the wallpaper into accordion pleats along the scored lines. Using the hole punch, make a hole at the centre of each fold, 1cm (⅜in) down from the top edge of the shade – this is easiest if you punch through a folded pleat.

Glue the short sides of the shade together, with the narrow end pleat tucked underneath.

3 FITTING THE FRAME

Thread the needle with cord elastic. Hold the lampshade over the frame. Thread the elastic through two holes, then over the ring, behind a pleat in the paper shade. Thread the elastic back through two holes and over the ring again. Continue binding the ring to the shade until you get back to the starting point. Knot the ends of the elastic together inside the shade and trim the ends.

4 ADDING THE RIBBON TRIM

Thread the ribbon through the punched holes, concealing the elastic. Tie the ribbon in a neat bow on the front of the shade. Trim the ends.

UMBRELLA STAND

STENCIL TEMPLATE

With our unreliable weather what could be more fitting in a hall than an umbrella stand. An old terracotta chimneypot makes a convenient and original umbrella stand. This one was given a face-lift with woodstain, gold paint and a smart stencil design.

DECORATING THE CHIMNEYPOT

Paint the chimneypot with dark woodstain, then highlight the top edge with gold paint. Trace the motif from the template (above) and make a stencil. Use a small sponge to stencil the motif at regular intervals around the base of the pot. Place a large plastic flowerpot saucer inside the chimneypot to catch the drips from wet umbrellas.

Mellow Moods Hall

If a Classical Look hall is too formal for you, discover the versatility of a mellow style with two easy looks for your hall, using either warm or cool colours. In this project, find out how to combine earth tones, wood and matching accessories.

In this room you can make:
- Realistic stained-glass effects
- Decorated fingerplates
- Painted wooden or metal accessories

◀ Paint a wooden platter to go on a hall table.

▶ Be creative with colour and have a light and elegant look with cool aqua and grey.

WARM YELLOW HALL

This version of the hallway is reminiscent of the Edwardian era, yet it's right up to date. The strong, glowing colours – terracotta, gold and cream – and the warm tones of natural woods are practical for a busy traffic area like this, and they create a warm and welcoming atmosphere.

The focal point is the stained-glass door – you can create this effect with special plastic film. Other important features are the stripped pine dado rail, door frames and staircase, and the unusual painted sideboard and oak settle. Framed botanical prints, and brass door and light fittings add complementary touches.

Your hallway colour scheme will work best if the adjoining rooms are decorated in complementary colours, so that your eye follows through in an easy, natural way. So for these rooms, consider other warm or spicy shades, or paler versions in patterns or plains. Warm-toned neutrals and natural shades would also work well.

STAINED-GLASS

You can give plain glass panels on your front door the look of stained-glass by using a special 'peel and stick' plastic film. You can buy the plastic film by mail order.

Follow the steps here for basic know-how. For more detailed and technical advice, it is advisable to follow the manufacturer's instructions.

▼ Cut botanical motifs from cards or wrapping paper and stick them on to plain paper, cut to the same size as a clear fingerplate. Fix the paper behind the fingerplate when you attach it to the door.

▼ Use 'peel and stick' stained-glass effect borders to add a designer touch to a straight-sided plain glass vase. You can also use the borders around the edges of stained-glass effect panels on windows and glazed doors to add a neat finishing touch.

MATERIALS

One or two stained-glass panel designs on plastic film

Matching grid sheet (optional)

Steel measuring tape

Ruler

Pencil

Sharp craft knife

Scissors

Protective cutting surface

Methylated spirits

Lint-free rag

Soapy water and a cloth

Small piece of strong card

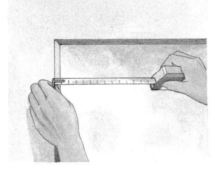

1 MEASURING UP
Measure the glass to be decorated. This will help you to plan your design and match up the main grids and border strips. Lay the stained-glass panel flat on your protective cutting surface and transfer the measurements on to it with a ruler and pencil.

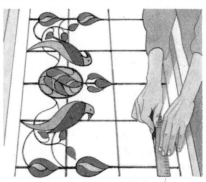

2 CUTTING THE DESIGN
Cut the design to size, allowing a little extra all round for trimming. The trimming allowance enables you to fit the design accurately later. Use a ruler and craft knife to cut straight lines, and use scissors to cut round curves.

3 PREPARING THE GLASS
Wipe over the glass with methylated spirits and a lint-free rag to remove any surface dirt and grease. Using a cloth, cover the entire area of glass with soapy water. This will make it easier to slide the stained-glass panel into position. You will also find the panel easier to apply if the glass is cool and out of direct sunlight.

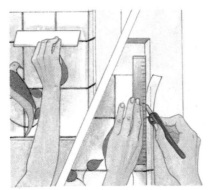

4 POSITIONING THE PANEL
Peel away the backing sheet and position the design over the soapy glass. Wet the front with soapy water. Use the piece of card to smooth the panel from the centre outwards, squeezing out the soapy water and any air bubbles which may have formed. Then stand back and check the position of the design. If it isn't quite right, simply peel it off and re-position it. Trim the excess material away carefully with a craft knife.

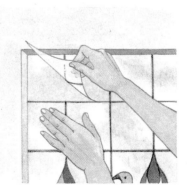

5 FITTING EXTRA GRIDS
Although the panel designs are generously sized, you may need to add an extra area of grid, particularly if you have altered the panel proportions to achieve a special effect, such as positioning the motif at the base of the glass. To fill in around the panel, measure and cut the grid sheet and apply it in the same way as the main panel, matching up the grid lines.

PAINTED PLATTER

A convenient place to sling your keys is an asset in a hall. The simple pattern on this wooden platter was inspired by the design painted on the hall sideboard. Try this small project first, before using the same technique to decorate a larger item such as a piece of furniture.

MATERIALS

Wooden platter

Fine sandpaper

Finest gauge wire wool

Emulsion paint in cream and coffee

Wood stain in four wood tones, ranging from light to dark

Small household paintbrush

Flat artists' watercolour brush

Lint-free rag

Dishes for mixing paint

Small dishes for the wood stain

Tracing paper and masking tape

Pencil and ruler

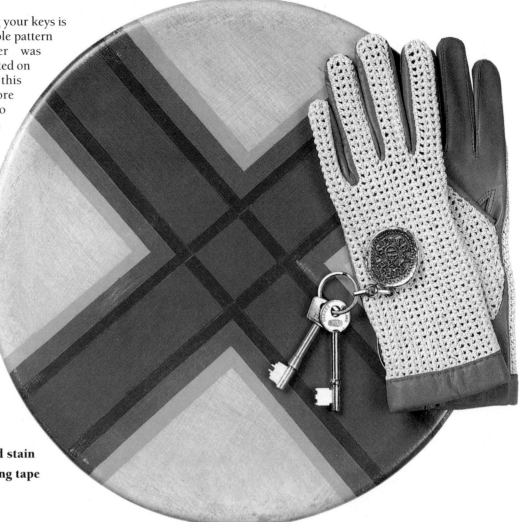

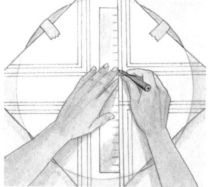

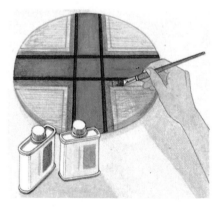

1 PREPARING THE WOOD
Rub the wooden platter lightly with sandpaper to provide a key for the paint. Pour a little cream emulsion into a container and mix it with water to a watery consistency. Using the household paintbrush, brush on a coat of this wash, and leave it to dry. Then thin the coffee emulsion to a very watery consistency. Dab the rag into this and rub it well into the painted surface to 'antique' the colour.

2 MARKING THE DESIGN
Draw round your platter on to tracing paper and mark the centre point. Using a ruler and pencil, copy the pattern on the platter pictured above on to the tracing paper. Place the tracing, drawing side down, on the platter and hold it in place with masking tape. Using the pencil, draw over the lines again to transfer them on to the surface. If your platter is flat, use a ruler to help to keep the lines straight.

3 PAINTING THE DESIGN
Pour a little of the third darkest wood stain into a dish. Using the flat-tipped watercolour brush, paint on the central, widest lines, and leave them to dry. Then paint on the thin, darkest lines and leave them to dry. Paint on the second darkest wood stain in the same way, and finally paint the lightest, outer lines. When the wood stain is completely dry, gently rub over the surface with fine sandpaper to distress the wood. Finally, use the wire wool to buff the surface to a sheen.

Mellow Moods Hall – Cool colours

Clear, clean lines and cool, contrasting colours give this modern hall its elegant look. Team pale shades of aqua with grey to create a spacious feeling, and add dark metal accessories for a smart, modern accent.

▼ **This interpretation of the Mellow Moods hall shows how alternative colours and textures – aqua and grey with metal – creates a different look.**

COOL AND ELEGANT HALL

This version of the Mellow Moods hall provides a cool, elegant look. The clear colours give it a spacious, uncluttered feel, and the clean lines of the furniture and accessories add a modern twist which balances the traditional elements, such as the stained-glass door and dado rail.

The walls are pale aqua, with Anaglypta wallpaper under the dado rail for a subtle change of texture. The woodwork is painted in palest grey and deep aqua, and the flooring is a practical, dark, mottled grey.

This subtle colour scheme provides the perfect backdrop for the interesting shapes of the cast-iron furniture. You can recreate this look instantly by painting wood or metal furniture and accessories with metallic paints.

For inexpensive prints that look antique, you can make black and white photocopies of favourite subjects, such as period illustrations of plants or wildlife. Reduce or enlarge them to the size you need. If you like, you can tint the photocopies with a wash of artists' ink to give them greater depth, and découpage them on accessories, such as an umbrella stand.

GATHERED GUSSET CUSHION

Dress up a round box cushion with contrast piping and a gathered gusset. The piping gives a crisp line, while the gathered gusset softens the shape. This cushion is made in a similar way to a basic round box cushion, but it has an interlining, and the gusset doesn't have a zip.

MATERIALS

Round box cushion pad

Black fabric (see steps 1 and 2 for the amount)

White fabric-covered piping

Pre-shrunk calico for interlining (see step 1 for the amount)

Matching sewing thread

Buttonhole twist

Paper for a pattern

1 PREPARING THE TOP AND BASE
Make a paper pattern for the cushion top and base. Cut a cushion top and base from black fabric, and a cushion top and base from calico for the interlining. Tack a calico circle to the wrong side of each black circle. Tack piping around the edges of the top and base, snipping into the seam allowance at intervals for ease, as necessary.

2 CUTTING OUT THE GUSSET
Measure the depth of the cushion pad and add on 3cm (1¼in) for seam allowances. Then measure the circumference, double it and add 3cm (1¼in) for seam allowances. Cut a strip of black fabric to these measurements, joining lengths as necessary.

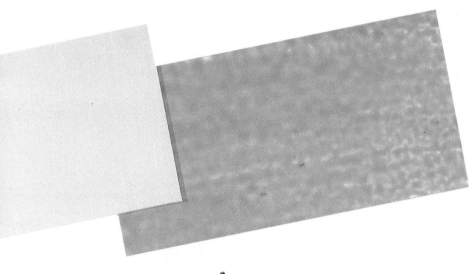

◄ Paints in cool shades of aqua give the hall a fresh look and help to create a spacious feeling. Grey metallic paint, used on the chair, mirror frame and wire basket, adds a smart modern accent.

◄ Use dark grey metal paint to make a simple wire basket into an impressive 'cast-iron' accessory.

► This striking chair started out as an ordinary white, plastic-coated garden chair, but a coat of grey metal paint has given it a chic new look. Add a smartly piped black and white cushion to create a decorative and useful piece of furniture for your hall.

3 MAKING THE GUSSET

With the right sides together, pin and then stitch the short ends of the gusset strip to make a loop. Press the seam open. Using strong thread, such as buttonhole twist, run two rows of gathering stitches along the seamline on both long edges. Pull up the gusset to fit the cushion top and base.

4 COMPLETING THE CUSHION

With the right sides together, pin and stitch the gusset to the top and base pieces, leaving a large gap along one edge. Snip into the seam allowances all round at intervals for ease. Turn the cushion cover to the right side, insert the cushion pad and slipstitch the opening closed.

DECOUPAGED UMBRELLA STAND

As in the previous Classical Look hall project, an umbrella stand provides the perfect opportunity for making a useful and decorative accessory for any hall. Make this stylish umbrella stand from a metal florists' container.

MATERIALS

Tall metal container

Grey metal paint

Manufacturer's brush cleaner

Household paintbrush

Photocopy prints in two sizes

Spray adhesive or wallpaper paste

Black Indian ink

Small dish

Artists' watercolour brush

Small curved scissors

Matt, colourless varnish

1 PAINTING THE CONTAINER
Make sure the container is clean and dry, and remove any flaky paint or rust. Using the household paintbrush, paint it inside and out with grey metallic paint, and leave it to dry.

2 COLOURING THE PRINTS
Choose enough photocopy prints to make a decorative band to go roughly half way up the container – enlarge them if necessary. Reduce some more to make a decorative band round the top of the container. Dilute a little black Indian ink with water in a small dish, then paint this over the photocopies, using the watercolour brush. You can make the prints as dark or as light as you wish by adding more ink or water. Leave the prints to dry.

3 GLUING ON THE PRINTS
Use small scissors to cut out the motifs, cutting as close to the printed edge as possible. Try out their positions on the container, then stick each one in place with spray adhesive or wallpaper paste. Smooth the paper flat and leave it to dry. Protect the paper motifs with a coat of varnish, brushing it out lightly to cover the edges of the motifs.

▶ The photocopies used to decorate this metal container were taken from stickers, but you could use wrapping paper, old illustrations or cards.

▲ This eye-catching mirror frame was made by gluing a square of blue-painted hardboard on to a larger square of metal-painted hardboard. Mount a mirror in the centre.

Mellow Moods Sitting Room

You'll probably spend a great deal of your free time in your sitting room – so make it somewhere that you can feel relaxed. Soft colours, pretty furnishings and informal accessories give a fresh feel. It's a look that's easy to achieve.

▼ Give your sitting room a light and airy feel with softly stippled walls, two-tone stencils and matching soft furnishings and accessories.

Paint plain storage boxes in colours to match your room scheme.

Work this attractive cushion panel in half cross stitch.

Make a découpage vase using colourful scraps of foil.

A FRESH LOOK

Delicate colours, pretty paint effects and dainty decorative details give this sitting room its fresh and airy feel. It's based on a palette of soft purples and blues with yellow and cream providing a gentle balance. You can create a similar look with other soft colour mixes – try peach with mint green and cream, or pink with blue and cream.

The walls in the picture were painted in buttery yellow and then stippled in soft mauve. You could use a mottled wallpaper instead, or a speedy paint effect, like rag rolling or sponging. Repeat the effect on accessories, like a planter, boxes and trays.

Add pattern to the painted walls with stencils, choosing motifs which tie in with the fabric designs. Soften simple accessories such as plain lampshades with matching stencils.

Informal decorations make a room feel more relaxed, so introduce some softly draping fabrics, such as a one-piece curtain swag. Cover your sofa and armchairs in loose covers and add soft, patterned cushions.

STENCILLED MOTIFS AND BORDERS

Stencils make it easy to add decorative touches to painted walls and to create coordinating accessories.

Take a tip from the stencilled designs in this sitting room, and choose a motif that's available in different sizes – this will give you scope to decorate a whole range of different surfaces. Alternatively, make your own stencils, tracing the design from your fabric – you can enlarge or reduce it on a photocopier to get exactly the size you want.

Choose just one colour for the stencil, then create a two-tone effect by dabbing it lightly with a stronger shade of the same colour. The easiest way of obtaining two shades of the same colour is to start with the darker shade and then add a little white to it to create the lighter shade.

STENCILLED BORDER

The stencilled border was created by positioning the motif level with the curtain track. You can copy this effect, or you may prefer to line up the motif with another feature like a mantelpiece or picture rail. Alternatively, you can create a cornice effect along the top of the walls, or decorate the skirting boards and around the door and window frames, or stencil a dado effect at waist height round the walls.

MATERIALS
Stencils
Spray adhesive and solvent
Small pieces of fine sponge
Plate or saucer for mixing
Scrap paper
Paint in two shades of mauve
Ruler, pencil and eraser
Spirit level

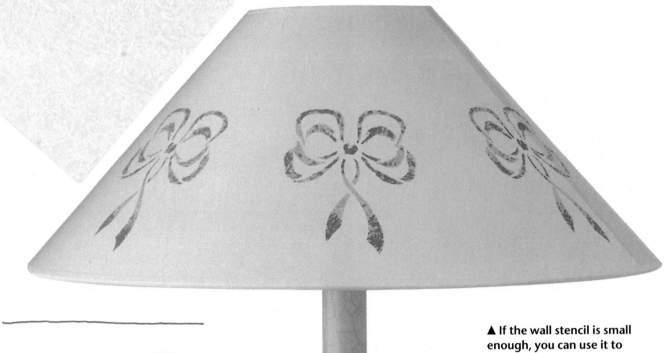

▲ If the wall stencil is small enough, you can use it to to stencil accessories, such as this lampshade. Use ordinary emulsion paint or fabric paint in coordinating colours.

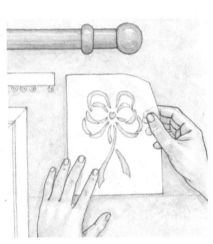

1 STENCILLING THE DESIGN

Starting close to the curtain pole (or other key feature), measure and mark the positions for the stencil with the pencil and ruler. Mix a little of the lighter paint in the saucer, dip the sponge into it, then dab off the excess on scrap paper. Use spray adhesive to hold the stencil at the starting point, then dab the sponge through the stencil. Leave the paint to dry, then remove the stencil and reposition it as required, using the spirit level to check the positioning if necessary. Repeat until the border is complete.

2 CREATING TWO TONE EFFECTS

Mix a little of the darker paint on a saucer and dip the sponge into it. Dab off the excess paint on scrap paper. Position the stencil over the previously stencilled design and then use the sponge to dab a little colour over selected areas. For a ribbon bow, like the one in the picture, add the paint on the twist of the ribbon and the knot.

▲ Adequate storage space is a perennial problem – why not make some storage boxes that are both pretty and practical. These boxes have been stippled to match the sitting room walls. Both boxes were painted with a base coat of warm, buttery yellow. The smaller box was stippled with the same pale mauve as the walls, and the larger box was stippled with a deeper mauve to create a subtle colour variation.

▶ This elegant tieback gathers the curtain into softly draping folds. The design echoes the pattern on the cushions. It's worked on canvas in half cross stitch in coloured yarns which coordinate with the curtains.

Mellow Moods Sitting Room – Tapestry cushions

Add a stylish valance to update the look of an armchair cover – choose a colour that matches the walls or curtains in your sitting room. Add a cushion with an embroidered inset, and continue the floral theme with a picture made from pressed-flower cards.

▼ These colourful tapestry cushions add decorative detail to the living room. You could create a similar effect with a mixture of patterned fabric cushions.

CHAIR COVER

Give your armchair a fresh new look with a valanced loose cover in a fabric which coordinates with your new decorations. Trim an existing cover with a smart piped valance to link it with the other soft furnishings in the room. The valance has neat mock pleats for ease of fit over each chair leg.

MATERIALS

Furnishing fabric for the valance

Fabric-covered piping cord to go round the base of the chair and for any other piped details

Lining fabric

Heavyweight sew-in interfacing

Long zip for the cover and a zip for the cushion

Matching sewing threads

Pins and a tape measure

Paper to make a pattern

Dressmakers' marker pen

1 MAKING THE VALANCE PATTERN
Decide on the depth of the valance: 10-18cm (4-7in) is standard. With the cover on the chair, measure from the floor to the top of the valance (**a**), and mark the position on the chair with the dressmakers' marker pen.

Measure the width across the front of the chair (**b**), the side (**c**) and the back (**d**). Add 3cm (1¼in) to each width for side seams and 3cm (1¼in) to the depth for seams. Cut paper patterns to these measurements.

For the pleat inserts, cut a paper rectangle 19cm (7½in) wide by twice the valance depth plus 3cm (1¼in).

2 FORMING THE MOCK PLEATS
Use the paper patterns to cut one front, one back and two side valance pieces from main fabric, interfacing and lining. Cut four pleat rectangles from main fabric. With the right sides facing, stitch the pleat rectangle ends together to make four loops. Fold each loop in half to enclose the seam.

3 LINING THE VALANCE PIECES
For each valance piece, pin the interfacing to the wrong side of the main fabric, then pin the fabric to the lining with right sides facing. With the lining on top, stitch around the sides and base taking 1.5cm (⅝in) seams. Clip the corners and turn out the fabric.

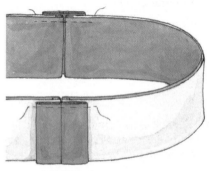

4 ATTACHING THE MOCK PLEATS
Arrange the valance pieces together end to end in order. Pin a pleat insert behind the butted ends, with the raw edges matching and the pleat seam at the back. Tack across the top raw edges through all the layers.

5 ADDING THE PIPING
Starting at a back corner pleat, pin and tack the piping to the right side of the valance, with the right sides together and the raw edges matching.

6 ATTACHING THE VALANCE
Take the cover off the chair. With the right sides facing, pin the valance to the marked line on the cover along the tacking for the piping. Tack the valance in place, then machine stitch the seam. Neaten the seam allowances with zigzag stitch, then turn the cover out and press it. Remove the tacking.

PRESSED FLOWER PICTURE

Pressed flower cards are attractive keepsakes. Keep them on permanent display by framing them as pictures.

Choose a picture frame large enough to allow a generous border round the cards. Four 18 x 12.5cm (7 x 5in) cards were used in the picture on a 48 x 38cm (19 x 15in) mount.

MATERIALS

Four pressed flower cards, all the same size

Mounting card

Craft knife and metal rule

Ruler and set square

Pencil and eraser

Masking tape

Picture frame

Cutting mat or protective surface

▼ Two tiebacks, hanging from a hook, make a simple and effective frame for the flower picture.

1 POSITIONING THE CARDS
Remove the picture frame glass and place it on the mounting card. Draw round the edge. Mark the centre at the top and base, and lightly mark a vertical line between the marks. To create a good visual balance, the picture mount should have an outer border that is slightly deeper at the base than the sides – 1.2cm (½in) is usual. With this in mind, arrange the four cards evenly on the mount on each side of the vertical line.

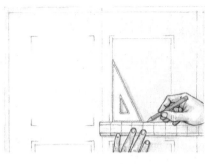

2 MARKING THE WINDOWS
When you are satisfied with the effect, mark the corners of each card lightly on the mounting card, and remove the cards. Using the ruler and set square, draw the window shapes 6mm (¼in) inside the marked corners.

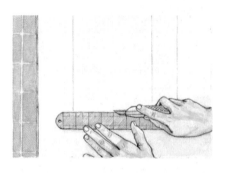

3 CUTTING THE MOUNT
Using the metal ruler and craft knife, cut the mount along the outer drawn lines on a protective surface.

Cut out the windows with bevelled edges: position the metal rule on the drawn line; hold the knife at 45 degrees to the surface and, starting at one corner, draw the knife evenly against the rule. Cut down to each corner, pressing the tip of the blade firmly into the mount at this point.

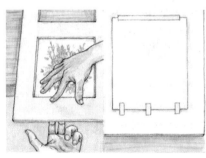

4 MOUNTING THE CARDS
Place one card, right side up, on the edge of a table, and position the mount on top. Holding the mount and card steady, reach under the edges and attach two or three pieces of masking tape to hold the layers together. Turn the mount over and secure the edges neatly with masking tape. Repeat for the other cards, then fit the mount into the frame.

EMBROIDERED CUSHION PANEL

Cushions provide an ideal focal point to large expanses of upholstery on a sofa or large armchair Stitch this little canvaswork panel to the centre of a plain fabric cushion cover, or make it into a tiny scented cushion, padded with pot pourri. The finished panel is 15cm (6in) square.

MATERIALS

25cm (10in) square of white lockweave canvas with 12 holes per 2.5cm (1in)

Anchor Tapisserie wool in the shades and amounts listed in the key

Tapestry needle, size 20

Tapestry frame (optional)

Matching sewing threads

Plain square cushion cover

Square cushion pad

MAKING THE CUSHION PANEL

Mount the canvas in the tapestry frame (optional). Following the chart (below), stitch the design in half cross stitch. Remove the canvas from the frame and press it. Trim the edges of the panel to 1cm (⅜in), turn these under and pin them in place. Slipstitch the panel to the centre of the cushion cover.

KEY

☐	white 8004 – 1 skein		=	pale lilac 8602 – 1 skein
·	cream 8036 – 1 skein		⁄	lilac 8606 – 1 skein
÷	yellow 8016 – 1 skein		×	purple 8612 – 1 skein
℗	pink 8362 – 1 skein		•	royal blue 8692 – 2 skeins

Mellow Moods Sitting Room – Window treatments

Make softly draping swags and tails to frame the curtains in your sitting room, and paint a wooden curtain pole to match. For added appeal, paint a plain planter in a fresh colour and then stencil it with the same design as you used on the walls.

▼ **Informal swags and tails give the curtains a neat finish and emphasize the shape of the window. The warm yellow lining is revealed on the tails.**

INFORMAL SWAGS AND TAILS

This elegant swags and tails treatment is perfect for the windows of your Mellow Moods sitting room, where the emphasis is on using colour and soft furnishings to create an informal feel.

These swags and tails are made by draping fabric over a curtain pole fixed above the curtains. Choose a fabric with a pattern which looks good whichever way you hang it – stripes, spots, checks and other strong geometric patterns work well. A one-way pattern, such as a large floral, would hang upside down on one side of the swag. Choose a plain, toning lining which will help to emphasize the fabric drapes and folds, and create a subtle sense of movement.

MATERIALS

Main fabric (see step 3 for the amount)

Lining fabric (see step 3 for the amount)

Wooden curtain pole with finials, 40cm (16in) longer than the curtain track

Self-adhesive touch-and-close fastening such as Velcro Stick N' Stick, the same length as the curtain pole

Matching sewing thread

String

Tape measure

Long ruler

Dressmakers' marker pen

1 POSITIONING THE POLE
Hang the curtains and fix the pole about 15cm (6in) above the curtain track, so that it extends 20cm (8in) on each side.

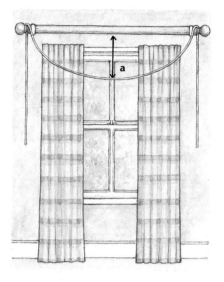

2 MEASURING UP
Loop a piece of string across the pole to decide how deep the swag should be and how long to make the tails: the swag should be no deeper than one sixth of the window drop, and the tails should fall halfway to two thirds of the way down each side of the window. Measure the depth of the string across the window at its fullest point (**a**), then measure its full length.

3 CUTTING OUT THE FABRIC
Cut a length of main fabric and lining the length of the string plus 3cm (1¼in). If your window is small, or the fabric is heavy, you may need to trim off some of the fabric width to avoid an over-full effect.

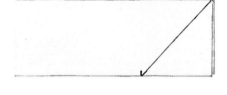

4 SHAPING THE FABRIC
Fold the main fabric in half widthways with the right sides together. To shape the tail ends in proportion to the swag depth, start at the short, raw edges and measure along one long edge to the same depth as the swag. Mark the fabric at this point. Using the dressmakers' pen and long ruler, mark a diagonal line from here to the nearest opposite corner. Cut along the line through both fabric layers. Repeat with the lining fabric.

5 SEWING THE SWAGS AND TAILS
Pin the lining to the main fabric with the right sides facing. Stitch all round them, taking 1.5cm (⅝in) seam allowances and leaving a gap in the longest edge to turn the fabric through. Trim the seam allowances at the corners, turn the fabric right sides out and slipstitch the gap closed. Press the fabric neatly.

6 HANGING THE FABRIC
Separate the touch-and-close fastening strip. Stick one part to the top of the pole. Drape the fabric over the pole, arranging the folds as desired. Pin and then stitch the fabric folds in place, if required. When you are satisfied with the effect, stick the remaining part of the touch-and-close tape to the lining side of the drape, and press it to the strip on the pole.

PAINTED CURTAIN POLE

A decorated wooden curtain pole, painted to coordinate with the curtain fabrics, looks very effective with informal swags and tails.

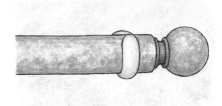

Rub over the pole with fine sandpaper and wipe it down. Paint the pole to match the walls or furnishing fabric, using a paint suitable for wood. For a mottled effect, like the one shown here, lightly stipple the pole, using a light colour paint for the base coat and a darker colour over the top. You can pick out details, such as the brackets or any mouldings on the pole finials, using a small paintbrush dipped in one or two contrast colours.

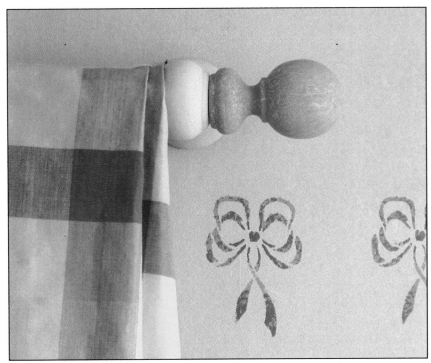

► Transfer an outdoor planter into a smart indoor accessory by painting and stencilling it to match the decor. To copy this idea, paint the planter to match the walls or woodwork, then stencil motifs on the sides in a contrasting colour, to echo the wall designs.

Here, the planter is used to contain a lavender bush which matches the yellow and blue decor, but you could use any flowering or foliage plant that you find particularly attractive – or easy to keep.

FOIL DECOUPAGE BOWL

You can create a lustrous design in a plain glass bowl or vase by covering the inside with pieces of coloured foil. Sweet wrappings are ideal for this form of découpage – they're easy to collect and are available in a variety of colours and textures.

Stick on the foil scraps with spray adhesive, which produces a fine, sticky mist. You can buy spray adhesives from art shops.

MATERIALS

Glass bowl

Coloured foils

Spray adhesive and solvent

Sharp craft knife or scissors

Tweezers (optional)

Metallic paint suitable for glass and ceramics or enamel paint and solvent

Small paintbrush

Paper tissues

Old newspapers to protect the work surface

1 PREPARING THE FOILS
Smooth the foils flat, discarding any with nicks and flaws, and cut out a selection of squares and triangles, taking care not to damage the edges. To try out different effects, hold the foil shapes inside the vase with your fingertips – position small shapes first, with larger ones behind.

2 ATTACHING THE FOILS
Make sure the glass is clean and dry. Lightly spray adhesive on the inside of the bowl over a small area near the base. Using tweezers or your fingers, put the foils in place, overlapping the edges slightly; press them flat. Leave them to dry slightly, then gently remove any excess sticky mist with a solvent-dampened tissue. Check that the foil shapes are flat.

3 COMPLETING THE DESIGN
Continue building up the design to the rim of the vase. Leave a small, uncovered area around the rim, so that the backing paint can cover the foil edges. Spray the backs with adhesive. Gently press larger pieces of foil on top for extra protection. Leave them to dry.

4 PAINTING INSIDE THE VASE
Using the small paintbrush, apply a layer of metallic or enamel paint carefully over the back of the foil, and paint neatly around the rim of the bowl. Leave the paint to dry completely, then add a second coat of paint and leave it to dry.

Black & White Sitting Room

If you want to make a definite design statement in your sitting room, nothing is more dramatic than choosing black and white. Introduce an accent colour, such as vibrant blue, for a key piece of furniture, then add colour-matched accessories.

In this room you can make:
- Block-print patterns
- Découpage table
- Graphic picture mounts
- Rosette curtain trims
- Black and white cushions

Create stylish picture mounts using wallpaper borders.

Make these graphic black and white papier mâché bowls.

Stitch a canvaswork design as a beautiful cushion insert.

CREATING THE BLACK AND WHITE SCHEME

Black and white is a timeless colour combination that can be adapted to suit many decorating styles. Its striking simplicity makes it an ideal choice for a sitting room decorated in a contemporary style, where bold good looks and clearly defined lines are integral elements.

Choose a rich accent colour, like the bright blue shown on the previous page, to lift and soften the scheme, and to add interest. Jewel green, acid green, deep red or brilliant yellow are all colours that would combine well with black and white.

Paint your walls in black and white, then design a block-print motif to create a patterned dado. Mix black and white stripes, checks and toning plains together to make cushions and picture mounts, and then carry the theme through with quick and easy curtain and lampshade trims. You can also decorate papier mâché bowls and a small table with black and white paper shapes cut from wallpaper.

DECOUPAGE TABLE

Create a unique découpage design on a small, inexpensive white table, using black and white stripes and other bold, geometric patterns cut from wallpapers and borders.

MATERIALS

Small, square, white medium density fibreboard (MDF) table

Black and white striped wallpaper

Coordinating wallpaper border

PVA adhesive

Decorators' colourless acrylic varnish in a dead flat finish

Small household paintbrush

Tape measure

Ruler, set square and pencil

Scissors

Craft knife, cutting edge and cutting surface

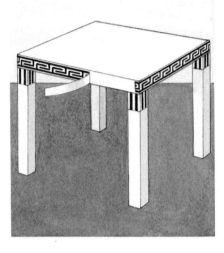

1 DECORATING THE TABLE LEGS
Measure round one of the legs and add 1cm (⅜in) for an overlap. Measure, mark and cut out four 9cm (3½in) deep strips to this size across the wallpaper, with the stripes running vertically. Spread adhesive evenly across the back of a strip, and stick it round the top of a table leg, placing it with the overlap at the inside corner of the leg. Smooth round, so that the strip end is in line with the inside edge of the leg. Repeat for the other legs.

2 ADDING THE BORDER
Measure round the table top and add a 1cm (⅝in) overlap. Cut a length of wallpaper border to this size. Measure the depth of the table top and, if necessary, use a craft knife to trim the border so that its depth measures at least 6mm (¼in) less than the depth of the table top. Spread adhesive evenly over the back of the border. With the border centred, lay the overlap round one corner of the table, then smooth it in place round the table sides.

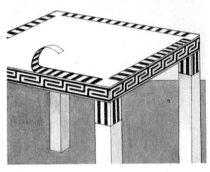

3 ADDING THE TOP STRIPES
Measure and mark 6cm (2¼in) out from each corner, on each side of the table top. Measure between the marks on one side and cut four 4cm (1½in) deep strips to this length from the striped wallpaper, cutting across the stripes. Spread adhesive evenly over the back of the strips, and smooth them down, in line with the table edge.

4 SEALING THE DESIGN
When the papers are completely dry, brush a coat of dead flat acrylic varnish over them to protect the surface. For an authentic découpage finish, paint the varnish over the entire table, then, when dry, repeat with another one or two coats to build up a durable finish.

PHOTOCOPIES *Tip*
You could reproduce black and white images on a photocopier, and use these to create découpage designs for your table. This would also enable you to enlarge or reduce the images as desired. As copy paper is thinner and more absorbent than wallpaper, you will need to protect both sides of the cut-outs with an acrylic spray sealant (from art shops) before you stick them in place.

▶ Transform an occasional table with a découpage design created using coordinating wallpapers.

PICTURE MOUNTS

Complement a black and white colour scheme by framing inexpensive greetings cards and postcards with impressive mounts. All you need are black and white striped wallpaper, a coordinating border and a bright, plain colour accent paper. Buy the cartridge and cover paper from art shops.

MATERIALS

One large and two small clip-back picture frames

Black and white striped wallpaper

Coordinating border

White cartridge paper

Accent colour (blue) cover paper

Greetings cards or postcards

Spray adhesive

Craft knife, cutting mat and metal straight edge

Ruler, pencil and set square

LARGE PICTURE MOUNT

1 PREPARING THE FRAME
Dismantle the frame. To make a backing for the picture, draw around the glass on to the white cartridge paper, and cut along the marked lines using a craft knife and cutting mat.

To frame a greetings card, cut away the back half along the crease line.

2 PLACING THE PICTURE
Use the ruler, pencil and set square to mark the position of the picture card centrally on the cartridge paper. Spray the back of the picture card with adhesive and stick it in place.

3 MAKING THE CORNER SQUARES
Measure the depth of the wallpaper border, and add 1.5cm (⅝in). Draw four squares to this size on the accent colour paper, and cut them out. Cut four border pieces to fit across the squares, then use spray adhesive to stick these centrally over the coloured squares. With the border patterns running horizontally, stick a square to each corner of the cartridge paper.

▼ Make simple postcards into a smart wall display with these dramatic picture mounts. They'll make chic accessories for your black and white scheme.

4 ADDING THE BORDER STRIPES
Measure the width and length of the cartridge paper, between the corner squares. Following the direction of the stripes, use a craft knife to cut two narrow strips of wallpaper to each measurement, with each strip showing a white stripe bordered by two black stripes. Measure the depth of one black stripe, and trim this amount off both ends of each strip. Stick each strip on to the cartridge paper, centred between the corner squares and in line with their inner edges, as shown. Reassemble the frame.

BORDER PATTERN MOUNT

Prepare the backing paper and picture card as for the LARGE PICTURE MOUNT, step 1, but using the accent colour paper for the backing. Measure the width and length of the backing paper and cut two strips of wallpaper border to each length; mark each measurement on the border before you cut it, and adjust them if necessary so that the pattern repeats are balanced on each piece. Stick the two side strips in place on the coloured paper, with edges level. Repeat for the top and base strips. Stick the print in the centre of the mount. Reassemble the frame.

SIMPLE STRIPED MOUNT

Remove the backing board, backing sheet and glass from the frame. Lay the striped wallpaper flat, and position the glass over this, so that the stripes run horizontally and are evenly positioned at the top and base. Cut round the glass with a craft knife. Use a ruler and pencil to mark the picture card position centrally on the stripes, then stick it in place with spray adhesive. Reassemble the frame.

Black & White Sitting Room – Curtain treatments

Paint the walls of your sitting room in dramatic black and white, then decorate the dado with a striking rope-effect print. For an elegant window dressing, drape filmy voile from a decorative pole, and trim it with black and white ribbon rosettes.

▼ Crisp, black and white ribbon rosettes add definition to these floaty, sheer drapes. The wrought iron pole and hold-backs add a stylish note.

ROPE-EFFECT BLOCK PRINTS

The black-painted dado in the black and white sitting room is decorated with a border print, created using a rope block stamp and contrasting white paint. To copy this look, all you need to do is glue short lengths of rope or thick cord on to strong card, roll a thin layer of paint over the rope, and then press the block to the wall.

If you prefer, you could create a softer effect on the same theme, with all-white walls, a contrasting black dado rail and skirting board, and a black rope-print border. Paint the walls with black and/or white emulsion paint, and leave them to dry thoroughly before starting to print your decorative border.

MATERIALS

14 x 11cm (5 ½ x 4¼in) piece of strong card

66cm (26in) of 1.5cm (⅝in) thick rope or cord

Epoxy resin glue (Araldite)

Black or white emulsion paint to contrast with the dado

Paint tray or dish

Small, household paintbrush

Small craft roller (available from art shops)

Pencil, ruler and craft knife

Masking tape and eraser

Scrap paper, such as old newspaper

▼ A rope-print border in white paint adds a decorative touch to this black dado rail.

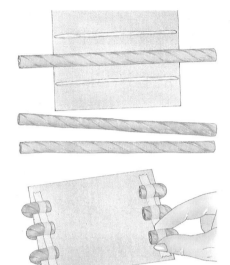

1 MAKING THE ROPE BLOCK
Cut the rope or cord into three equal lengths and seal the ends with glue to prevent unravelling. Measure and mark a centre line lengthways along the card. Draw a parallel line 2.5cm (1in) to each side of this. Run a line of prepared glue along the centre line, and press on a length of rope or cord, allowing an overlap at each end. Repeat to stick rope or cord over the other two lines. Turn the card over and glue the overlapping rope or cord ends to the back. Use masking tape to hold them in place until the glue sets.

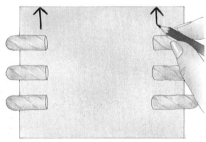

2 MARKING THE BLOCK
Mark one long edge of the card, on the wrong side, with pencilled arrows to show it is the top edge. Align this edge with the dado rail or guideline when printing the upper border, and the opposite card edge with the skirting board or guideline when printing the lower one.

3 PLANNING THE BORDERS

If there is no dado rail or skirting board, mark guidelines where you would like the borders to lie. Decide where to place your first print – centrally under a window or another focal point is ideal, or simply in one corner. Using the block and a pencil, measure and mark out from the first print, along the dado rail and skirting board or guidelines, to see how many whole prints will fit the space, allowing a 2-2.5cm (¾-1in) gap between each print; adjust the spaces slightly, as necessary, so that you finish with a whole print at corners. To fit the pattern around features, see step 5.

4 PRINTING THE BORDERS

Pour a little paint into the tray or dish. Use a paintbrush to apply a little paint to the roller. Run the roller across the rope block, coating it evenly with paint. Make a test print on scrap paper to see the effect, and to see how many clear prints you can make before reloading the brush – three is average. Re-apply paint to the block and start printing the wall, following the marked spacing and aligning the top or bottom edge of the card with the dado rail or skirting board, respectively, or with the guidelines.

PATTERN VARIATIONS *Tip*

Try making a second printing block, the same depth as the first one, but narrower. You can alternate this with the full-sized block to create interesting pattern variations. A narrower block is also a great asset if you have a lot of features to work round, as it will fit neatly into small spaces.

5 WORKING AROUND FEATURES

Camouflage small pattern mismatches at corners, and around features such as windows where the block does not fit, by printing two slightly overlapping motifs; when these are dry, simply paint a stripe of background colour across the two to create two slightly smaller motifs, which will blend in with the others.

When the borders are dry, use a clean eraser to remove any pencil marks from the wall.

▲ Papier mâché bowls are inexpensive and fun to make, and can look very dramatic – especially when decorated with bold colours and patterns.

Both of these bowls were made using strip papier mâché. They were given a base coat of white emulsion paint, then decorated to complement a black and white scheme, with découpage shapes cut from black and white striped and figurative wallpapers. You could also use photocopied images. Protect the bowls from wear and tear with a couple of coats of diluted PVA adhesive.

RIBBON ROSETTES

Trim the gathered heading of plain sheer curtains with chic black and white striped ribbon rosettes. Hold them in place with pins or a few stitches, for easy removal and cleaning. If you are hanging the curtains from a pole, make one rosette to correspond with each curtain ring.

MATERIALS

For each rosette:

50cm (20in) of 22mm (⅞in) wide, black and white striped grosgrain ribbon

Round, black button with shank, 2.5cm (1in) in diameter

Needle and matching sewing thread

Pearl-headed pin

1 SHAPING THE RIBBON
Cut the length of ribbon in half to make two 25cm (10in) lengths. Hold the centre of one length between your forefinger and thumb, and twist one ribbon end back on itself to the centre. Holding the centre securely, rotate the ribbon and twist in the other end to form a figure of eight, tucking it behind the centre. Hold the centre with a pin, then secure it with a few stitches. Turn the ribbon over and finger press the points flat. Repeat with the other ribbon length.

2 FORMING THE ROSETTE
With the pressed points facing up, put the two twisted loops together at right angles, matching the centres, to form a cross. Tuck in the uppermost raw ribbon end to a neat point, and anchor the cross at the centre with a few stitches. Stitch on the button, through all the ribbon layers. Repeat steps 1-2 to make the required number of ribbon rosettes.

3 ATTACHING THE ROSETTES
Use a pearl-headed pin at the back of each rosette to pin it to the gathered curtain heading, placing one below each curtain ring, if there are any. If not, simply space the rosettes an equal distance apart along the heading. Position each rosette with two of its points level with the curtain top.

Black & White Sitting Room – Patterned cushions

Choose black and white stripes, checks and matching plains to create comfortable soft furnishings for your sitting room. Stitch a beautiful, modern canvaswork design as a cushion insert, and trim a plain lampshade with coordinating striped ribbons.

▼ **Black and white cushions look dramatic grouped on a contrasting sofa. These are made from stripes and checks, and plain fabrics with canvaswork panels.**

CANVASWORK CUSHION

1 WORKING THE EMBROIDERY
Mount the canvas in the embroidery hoop, if you are using one. Following the chart on page 48 and using two strands of wool, work the central, figurative area and pointed roof in petit point over one canvas thread, except the white lines of the central tree, which are worked using three strands of wool over two canvas threads.

Work the design borders using four strands of wool over two canvas threads. Work the horizontal stripes in tent stitch, working the stitches in different directions on the white stripes, then stitch the remainder of the border in cross stitch. Remove the work from the hoop, if necessary, and press it gently into shape.

Work a modern, black and white cross stitch design, then frame it with a patchwork-style border to make a cushion for your black and white sitting room. The finished cushion measures 41cm (16in) square, with a 20cm (8in) canvaswork panel. The panel is embroidered in cross stitch and tent stitch. The tent stitch is worked over two canvas threads on the borders of the panel, and as petit point over one thread in the central area, to give a finer finish.

The measurements given for the black and white fabric borders include a 1.5cm (⅝in) seam allowance.

▲ Stitch a dramatic canvaswork design and frame it with bold black and white patchwork-style borders to make a striking cushion cover.

MATERIALS
Six skeins each of Appletons 2 ply crewel wool in white (992) and black (993)

25cm (10in) square of double cotton canvas with 10 holes to 2.5cm (1in)

Tapestry needle

50cm (⅝yd) black linen

20cm (¼yd) white linen

1.80m (2yd) black piping tape

Matching sewing threads

41cm (16in) square cushion pad

Embroidery frame (optional)

CUTTING LIST
From black linen
● Four 23 x 7.5cm (9 x 3in) strips
● Four 9cm (3½in) squares
For the cushion back:
● 44.5 x 30.5cm (17 ½ x 12in) rectangle
● 44.5 x 24.5cm (17½ x 9¾in) rectangle
From white linen
● Four 32.5 x 9cm (12¾ x 3½in) strips
● Four 7.5cm (3in) squares

2 ADDING THE INNER BORDER
With the right sides together and the edges matching, join a white linen square to each end of two black strips. Press the seams open and set aside. Placing each strip centrally, and with the right sides together, pin and stitch the remaining two black border strips on to each opposite side of the canvaswork panel, stitching close to the edge of the embroidery. In the same way, pin and stitch the black and white strips to the top and base edges of the panel, taking care to align the white square corners with the canvaswork corners. Press the seams away from the centre.

TRIMMED LAMPSHADE

3 ADDING THE OUTER BORDER
Follow the sequence in step 2 to stitch the outer border around the edges of the inner one, but reversing the colours. Press the seam allowances open as before.

4 PIPING THE EDGE
Starting halfway across a black corner square and working on the right side, pin the piping tape round the edges of the cushion front, with the tape edge level with the raw fabric edges. Stitch the tape in place, overlapping the ends neatly. Trim the piping ends level with the raw fabric edges.

Use black and white striped ribbon and silver metallic braid to jazz up a black lampshade on a contrasting white lampbase.

MATERIALS

A plain black straight-sided lampshade

Black and white striped Petersham ribbon, 22mm (⅞in) wide (see step 2 for quantities)

Black and silver Russia braid (see step 2 for quantities)

Clear craft glue

Tape measure, ruler and pencil

Needle and matching sewing thread

2 ESTIMATING FOR RIBBON
Measure the depth of the lampshade, and add 4cm (1½in) for turnings. Multiply this measurement by the number of marked strips to give the ribbon and braid amounts required. Cut the ribbon and braid into pieces of the required length.

3 TRIMMING THE RIBBON
Using backstitch and securing the thread at each end, stitch a length of Russia braid down the centre of each ribbon length.

5 MAKING UP THE CUSHION
Turn under 5mm (¼in) then 1cm (⅜in) along one long edge on each cushion back piece and stitch. Lay the cushion front flat with the right side facing up. Lay the smallest back piece over it, with the right sides together and the raw edges level. Lay the larger back piece alongside, with the raw edges level and the hemmed edges overlapping. Pin, tack and machine stitch all round through all layers, close to the piping edge. Clip the corners and turn the cover right side out. Insert the cushion pad.

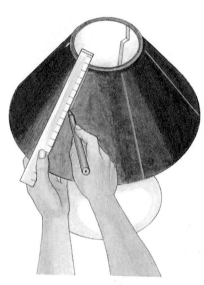

4 ADDING EACH RIBBON STRIP
Dab a little adhesive on to the wrong side of one end of a ribbon length and fold it under to stick. Run a thin line of adhesive down the centre back, then, when tacky, press the folded ribbon end over the shade top and along a drawn line on the shade. Neaten the lower end as at the top.

1 MEASURING UP
Mark the top of the shade at each side with a pencil, in line with the lamp carrier struts. These are the positions for the first two ribbon strips. To position strips in-between, measure the distance between the struts and divide this up, allowing for a space between each strip that is roughly equal to the ribbon width. Use a pencil to mark the position of the ribbons all round the top of the lampshade, then use a ruler and pencil to mark vertical lines to the lower edge.

▶ Strips of black and white ribbon and Russia braid give this plain black lampshade a chic finish. The trims are simply glued in place.

ADDING AN EXTRA BORDER *Tip*
Make an extra patchwork-style border for your cushion from black and white striped fabric, with white corner squares. For good proportions, cut the strips one-and-a-half times the depth of the existing borders.

CHART FOR CANVASWORK CUSHION PANEL

KEY

✗ cross stitch in black over two canvas threads

✗ cross stitch in white over two canvas threads

╱ tent stitch in black over two canvas threads

╱ petit point in black over one canvas thread

╱ tent stitch in white over two canvas threads

╱ petit point in white over one canvas thread

Classical Look Sitting Room

Warm, light colours and traditional fabrics give this room its classic feel. Find out how to recreate this look with softly sponged walls, a traditional dado-effect wallpaper border and coordinating accessories.

In this room you can make:
- A sponged wooden tray
- A decorative effect on your walls with sponging
- Wallpaper borders to add flair

Discover how to sponge-paint not just walls but home accessories too.

Make stylish tie-on curtains and pretty matching cushion covers.

Decorate plant pots and baskets with fabric wraps and bows.

A WARM-TONED THEME

This room, with its sponged yellow walls and bright curtains, would look cheerful even on the darkest day. The paint effect makes the room appear permanently bathed in a glow of sunshine, while the choice of wallpaper, matching border and curtain fabric gives the room a classic air, equally suitable for town or country.

The curtain treatment is classic with a modern twist, combining a traditional floral top curtain with a separate checked lining. Both are hung with ties from a wooden curtain pole which is sponged to match the walls. The accessories – tied cushion covers, fabric-wrapped pots and painted tray – provide pleasing design details with up-to-the-minute flair.

MAKING A SCHEME WORK

Combining floral patterns, geometric designs and textures like sponge paint effects can seem rather daunting, but if all these elements share a colour theme, planning a scheme around such ingredients can be a real delight.

These days fabric houses take all the hard work out of choosing matching paper and fabrics, by helpfully producing coordinating ranges. These can be used for walls and soft furnishings, leaving you scope to use your own individual 'finds' to complete the scheme.

The yellow living room puts this idea into practice – the curtains, wallpaper and wallpaper border are from a coordinated range, while the sponged wall, curtain pole and checked fabric add an individual touch.

The floral curtains, wallpaper and dado border in this sitting room are closely linked in scale and pattern. The prints offer a wide choice of accent colours – like the blue used to edge the curtain frill. Other items, such as the blue sponged tray and green sofa, repeat colours in the prints.

Follow these leads to create your own distinctive living room. The biggest decision will be which print range to use. Then just repeat the colours in the other furnishings and on the walls, as shown here.

A WOODEN TRAY

Try your hand at sponging by decorating a small object first – a tray is an ideal project to start with. Pick colours that will look good in your room – either use the same colours as those on the walls or ones that will tie in with the room. This tray is worked in three shades of blue emulsion paint, and protected with a coat of clear household varnish. You can also sponge with oil-based paints, in which case there is no need to add varnish.

MATERIALS

Silk or matt emulsion: mid blue for the base coat; lighter blue for the second coat, and blue-tinted white for the third coat

Primer (if the tray is new)

Shallow dish for paint

Household paintbrush

Natural or synthetic sponge – natural ones give best results

Plastic sheet / newspapers

Scrap paper for testing colours

Rags or kitchen paper for mopping up any spills

Rubber gloves (optional)

Clear polyurethane varnish (optional)

1 PREPARING THE TRAY SURFACE
If using a painted tray, remove any flaking paint and sand it smooth. If the tray is new, sand it, then apply a primer.

2 APPLYING THE BASE COAT
Using a paintbrush, apply the chosen base colour (mid blue). Paint the top of the tray and leave it to dry, then paint the base.

3 PREPARING TO SPONGE
Pour a little of the first sponging colour (pale blue) into a shallow dish. Dampen the sponge with water, then dip it into the paint. Squeeze it to remove excess paint.

SPONGING

Sponging is quick and easy, and gives a new look to plain walls, furniture and home accessories. It can also help to disguise uneven or imperfect surfaces.

The softly mottled effect is created by sponging one or more toning colour over a flat base colour, usually starting with the darkest colours and adding the lighter ones on top.

The most successful sponged effects create a subtle sense of depth. This is achieved by using a combination of two or three paint colours: contrasting colours look dramatic, while toning or complementary colours create a delicate finish. The results can be subtle or striking, depending on the colours you choose, the texture and size of the sponge and the pattern of sponge marks.

Sponging has a definite advantage over other paint techniques – if the finished item or wall appears too dark or too light, you can change the look by sponging over it with another colour. Before you start, test your chosen colours on a piece of scrap paper.

DECORATING A WALL

SPONGING A WALL

The wall in the picture was sponged with three complementary shades of yellow. To recreate this look, use the darkest shade for the base colour and sponge over it with the two lighter shades. Prepare the sponge, and apply the paint as for the wooden tray, keeping the pattern varied and working from the top of the wall downwards.

Afterwards, use the same shades of yellow to paint the curtain pole, preparing the wood in the same way as the tray. Finish with a protective coat of varnish.

USING BORDERS

Patterned wallpaper borders can effectively bring the decorations of a room together. In the picture above, a wide wallpaper border picks up the floral theme of the curtain fabric and repeats the strong yellow of the sponged walls.

The border is at dado rail height, about a third of the way up the wall. Placed here, a wide border can improve the proportions of a room – for example a high ceiling can be visually 'lowered'.

4 TESTING THE COLOURS
For the best effect, the sponge should be almost dry, so dab it on to a scrap of paper until it leaves a soft, mottled mark; if it is too wet the paint will smudge.

5 SPONGING THE FIRST LAYER
Lightly dab the sponge at random over the tray. Dab gently into the corners to avoid a colour build up. Turn the sponge as you work to vary the pattern.

6 APPLYING MORE COLOUR
Recharge the sponge with paint when necessary, removing the excess each time on scrap paper. Restart sponging in an inconspicuous place in case the new sponge mark blurs. Leave the paint to dry.

7 SPONGING THE SECOND LAYER
Using the blue-tinted white, start sponging as before. Fill in the gaps between the first sponged marks, and overlap some to blend the colours, taking care not to completely cover the base colour. Leave it to dry, then sponge over any areas again as desired.

Tip

SUCCESSFUL SPONGING
Try to avoid over-sponging in corners and at doors or windows where colour can build up. For these areas and around other awkward shapes, such as light fittings or plugs, the trick the professionals use is to work with a smaller sponge.

8 VARNISHING THE TRAY
Paint a thin coat of protective varnish – matt or gloss – over the top of the tray and leave it to dry before varnishing the underside.

SPONGED AND EMBROIDERED PICTURE

3 EMBROIDERING THE DESIGN
Use one strand of cotton and stem stitch to attach the fabric shapes. Add extra stem stitch lines around and on the flowers. Define the centres with small blocks of satin stitch, worked in two strands of cotton. Add a few extra blocks of satin stitch around the design. Back the embroidery with iron-on Vilene.

4 CUTTING THE FABRIC MOUNT
Back the mount fabric with iron-on Vilene, then lay it right side down. Centre the mount on top and draw around the outer and inner edges. Cut around the outer edges.

5 COVERING THE MOUNT
Glue the card mount to the wrong side of the fabric, so that it is in line with the outer drawn edges. Cut diagonally from corner to corner of the window area. Fold each triangle flap back and trim, then glue the flap down as shown.

Soft patches of watery paint, applied with a small sponge, form a pretty background for embroidery. You can take your inspiration from floral printed fabrics and customize the embroidery to coordinate with your furnishings.

Here, small pools of paint reflect the flowers in the print. Sheer ribbon and net, stitched at random over the painted areas, add depth to the 'floral' shapes. Details are added in stem and satin stitch.

▲ Highlight the link between your embroidery and furnishing fabrics by covering the card mount with a remnant of one of the fabrics.

MATERIALS

25 x 20cm (10 x 8in) piece each of cream cotton or linen background fabric and floral fabric

Water-based paint in three colours that match the floral fabric (use fabric paint or artists' acrylics)

Small piece of sponge

Stranded embroidery cottons in colours that match the fabric

Scraps of net and sheer fabric

50 x 20cm (20 x 8in) iron-on Vilene

25 x 20cm (10 x 8in) photo frame

Cardboard mount to fit the frame

Fabric glue, saucers and scrap fabric

Embroidery needle and pins

1 SPONGING THE COLOUR
Put some paint in a saucer and dilute it with water until it's runny. First practise dabbing the paint on to scrap fabric, then sponge three colours on the fabric, next to each other. Leave the fabric to dry.

2 ADDING EXTRA FABRIC SHAPES
Cut out small, irregular shapes from sheer and net fabrics. Position them on the painted areas, moving them until you are happy with the design, then pin them in place.

STEM STITCH

Work from left to right. Take a stitch forwards and a shorter one back so the thread emerges on the left of the previous stitch. Keep the thread under the needle for each stitch.

SATIN STITCH

Work parallel straight stitches close together. Bring the needle up again close to where it first went in, keeping the edge straight.

Classical Look Sitting Room – Bow-tied cushions

Bright tie-on curtains with separate linings will add a much-appreciated air of comfort to your living room. Make them to coordinate with the colour of the walls, and complete the effect with matching tie-on cushion covers.

▼Create pleasing window dressings with double tie-on curtains in contrasting fabrics. Then make a few cushion covers with pretty fabric ties.

TIE-ON CURTAINS

Both the curtains and separate linings have deep top hems gathered into a frill. On the floral top curtain the frill is edged with a contrasting band. The ties are arranged on the pole in alternate sequence so that the checked lining is clearly visible.

Both the curtain and lining are made in the same way, with a gathered heading tape to provide fullness behind the frill.

MATERIALS

Printed fabric

Plain fabric for contrast band

Checked fabric for lining

Complementary braid

Standard curtain heading tape

Matching sewing threads

Dressmakers' marker pen

CUTTING LIST

When measuring up for your curtains, add 40cm (15¾in) above the required curtain tape level for the top frill. For side and base hems add 5cm (2in). For a fashionable, luxurious look remember to allow extra fabric for pattern matching and sufficient fabric for each curtain to make a 'puddle' on the floor.

Cut all fabrics following the straight grain, unless otherwise stated.

For the contrast band on the print curtain, cut 10cm (4in) wide bias strips from plain fabric.

The matching curtain ties are spaced at 25cm (10in) intervals along the top of the heading tape. Work out how many ties you will need for each curtain, including the linings, and allow sufficient fabric to cut enough strips 51cm (20in) long and 12cm (4¾in) wide.

MAKING THE CURTAINS

Make the floral curtain and checked lining in the same way, but follow the relevant steps for adding the contrast band to the top frill or adding the edging braid.

1 STITCHING THE SIDES
Turn under double 2.5cm (1in) hems on the side edges of each curtain, including linings. To add a decorative braid along the leading edge, as on the checked lining, pin and topstitch the braid in place over the side stitching. Leave the braid unstitched at the lower edge until the hem is finished.

▼ The curtain and its separate lining are tied on to the curtain pole with fabric ties. The ties are arranged alternately so that the lining can be seen along the central leading edge.

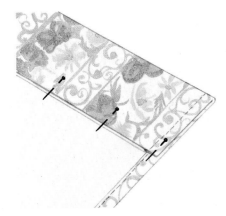

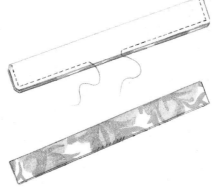

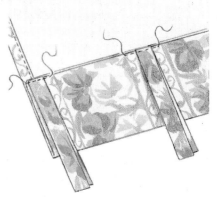

2 MARKING THE TOP FRILL

Mark the position for the curtain heading tape 40cm (15¾in) from the raw top edge, and fold the frill allowance over to the wrong side, level with this mark. Press along the fold line, and then pin the fabric layers together.

3 MAKING THE TIES

With right sides facing, fold the ties in half lengthways. Taking 1cm (⅜in) seams, stitch along the short and long edges, leaving a gap in the centre, as shown. Clip the corners and turn the ties right sides out. Slipstitch the gap closed. Press the ties flat.

4 ATTACHING THE TIES

Fold each tie in half widthways. With the wrong side of the curtain face up, pin each folded tie at regular intervals along the marked curtain tape position. When you are happy with the arrangement, tack the ties in place.

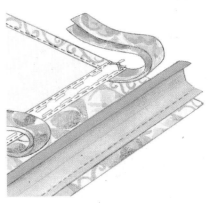

5 ADDING THE CURTAIN TAPE

With the wrong side of the curtain face up, pin and tack the tape (cords knotted securely at one end) over the raw edge of the frill and the tie folds. Machine stitch the tape in place.

6 FITTING A CONTRAST BAND

Join bias strips to the required length, then turn under 1cm (⅜in) along each long edge and press it in place. Fold the strip in half lengthways and press it. Working with the wrong side of the curtain face up, slip the band over the folded edge of the frill and mark the position of its folded edge, as shown.

7 STITCHING THE BAND

Open out the band and pin and stitch the folded edge along the marked line, leaving a small overlap at the sides, as shown. Turn the curtain over and slipstitch the other side of the band neatly in place. Push the side overlaps between the fabric folds and stitch to neaten them.

8 HANGING THE CURTAINS

Pull up the gathering cords on each curtain to the required fullness. Tie the curtain linings to the pole with double knots, making sure the curtains hang evenly. To hang the top curtains, position the first tie on the leading edge in between the first two ties on each lining, so that the leading edges of the linings are clearly visible. Check and mark the curtain hem levels, remove the curtains to stitch the hems, then hang them up as before.

TIE-ON CUSHION COVERS

These simple cushions are made from the same selection of plain, checked and patterned fabrics which were used for the curtains. Grouped together on a sofa or easy chair, they are classic accessories for a stylish yet comfortable living room.

MATERIALS

Fabrics: patterned, plain and check (for amounts see CUTTING LIST)

40cm (16in) square cushion pads

Matching sewing threads

▼ **Variation 1 (top) is made in one type of patterned fabric; variation 2 (centre) is made from checked fabric with a patterned central panel, and variation 3 (bottom) is made from plain fabric with contrast patterned side panels and ties.**

CUTTING LIST

Follow these instructions for covers to fit 40cm (16in) square pads, as here, or adapt the sizes to fit your existing cushions. 1.5cm (⅝in) seam allowances are included unless otherwise stated.

Variation 1
Cut two rectangles 42 x 48cm (16½ x 19in) for the front and back, and eight strips 18 x 25cm (7 x 10in) for the ties.

Variation 2
From checked fabric, cut out two rectangles 42 x 48cm (16½ x 19in) for the front and back, and eight ties 18 x 25cm (7 x 10in).
From patterned fabric, cut out a rectangle 23 x 48cm (9 x 19in) to make the central panel.

Variation 3
From plain fabric, cut two rectangles 42 x 48cm (16½ x 19in) for the front and back.
From patterned fabric, cut eight ties 18 x 25cm (7 x 10in) and two bands 14 x 48cm (5½ x 19in).

MAKING THE CUSHIONS

1 ADDING PANELS AND BANDS
For *variation 2* stitch the contrast panel, and for *variation 3* stitch the contrast bands to the cushion cover front. For each panel or band, fold under 1cm (⅜in) along the long edges and press them flat. Position each one as desired on the cover front, then pin and tack them in place. Machine topstitch close to the folded edge.

2 JOINING THE SIDE SEAMS
With right sides facing, stitch the two longest sides. Neaten seams as desired, turn right side out and press.

3 MAKING THE TIES
Fold each tie in half with right sides facing. Stitch across one end and down the side. Clip the corners and turn each tie right side out. Press the ties flat.

4 ATTACHING THE TIES
Lay the cushion cover flat and measure and mark 7.5cm (3in) in from each side on both unstitched seams. With the raw edges of the fabric level, pin each tie in line with these measurements. Measure and mark 4cm (1½in) in from the raw edge, and stitch each tie to the cover across these marks.

5 FINISHING OFF
Turn under the raw edges of the cover and ties for 1cm (⅜in) and stitch through all layers to neaten them. Fold in the open ends of the cover level with the tie stitching line, and press them flat. Insert a cushion pad and knot the ties in loose, double knots to hold the pad in place.

Classical Look Sitting Room – Pretty plant pots

Finishing touches make all the differences to a room – try making these pretty accessories. Fabric remnants turn a plastic plant pot into a stylish cache-pot. Trim a painted wicker basket with curvy stiffened fabric bows for added style.

▼ **Create decorative plant containers from ordinary pots. They are draped in glue-stiffened fabric and trimmed with bows that are also set with glue.**

STIFFENED BOWS

You can make stiffened bows with single or double loops to decorate small accessories such as picture frames and boxes, or make larger versions to trim plant containers, wicker baskets and hat boxes. Use the bows singly or group tiny ones in pairs, and add tails as desired.

Stiffened bows look good made from one fabric or two contrasting fabrics worked together – try a plain colour with a pretty print. You can use fabric oddments – choose fabrics to complement the background object by linking the colours in some way – or paint the object to blend with the fabric.

The instructions given here are for a double bow with tails. To make a single bow, or one without tails, just follow the instructions, leaving out unnecessary steps. Try out different effects before cutting the main fabric; measure the strips when you're pleased with the effect.

Note: the bow fabric is stiffened with a solution of PVA adhesive. You can buy plastic bottles of PVA adhesive in art shops.

MATERIALS

Light to mediumweight fabric

PVA adhesive

Measuring jug

Old mixing bowl

Rubber gloves

Old spoon

Florists' wire

Pins

Kitchen foil

Iron

1 CUTTING THE LOOPS
Decide on the size of your bow. To make a bow loop, cut a strip of fabric twice the width of the required bow, and add 1.2cm (½in) to the length for an overlap. Cut it twice the required depth of the bow, plus 6mm (¼in). For a double loop bow, cut another strip the same width as before, but make it about 4cm (1½in) longer than the first.

2 THE TAILS AND KNOT
To make the tails, cut a rectangle of fabric to the required length, and twice the bow depth. For the knot, cut a strip of fabric as for the bow loop, but half the width.

◄Give a new look to an ordinary wicker wastepaper basket by painting it in a fresh colour, such as cream or pastel blue, and adding a stiffened fabric bow. For a coordinated look, make the bow from the same fabric as your curtains or soft furnishings, or buy a fabric which picks up one of the main colours used in the other fabrics.

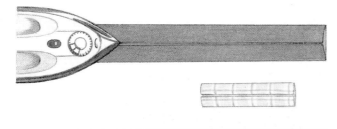

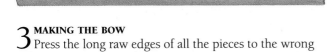

3 MAKING THE BOW
Press the long raw edges of all the pieces to the wrong side, to meet at the middle.

4 MIXING THE ADHESIVE
Mix one teacup of water and four of adhesive in the mixing bowl. Stir the mixture well with the spoon. Soak the fabric pieces in the adhesive and smooth off the excess with your hands. Fold each bow loop so that the short ends overlap slightly at the back. Squeeze the loops flat at the centre, and set them aside. Rinse out the bowl in water.

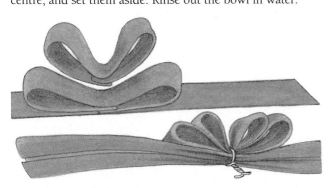

5 SECURING THE BOW
Lay the tail strip with its right side upwards, on a flat surface, and place the largest loop centrally on this, then place the smaller loop centrally on top. Wrap a piece of wire around the centre of the bow to gather it up. Twist the ends of the wire together at the back of the bow to secure it, and trim the ends.

6 FINISHING THE BOW
Wrap the knot strip around the centre of the bow, covering the wire, and overlap the ends together at the back, trimming the length as necessary. Secure the knot while it dries with a couple of pins. Ease the loops into shape, and hold them in place by pushing scrunched-up foil into them while the glue is drying. Leave the bow to dry in a warm room, and check it regularly to ensure it maintains its shape.

7 ATTACHING THE BOW
Stick the bow in place with undiluted PVA, and allow it to dry thoroughly. If necessary, use string or pins to hold the bow in place while the glue dries.

PROTECTING YOUR WORKSURFACE *Tip*
Protect your worksurface with a plastic sheet when doing particularly messy jobs, such as this one. You can buy cheap plastic sheets in DIY stores.

◀ Some bows look good on a small scale – especially on a little basket, like this. The bow transforms it from an ordinary wicker tray into a pretty serving dish for biscuits or petit four.

WRAPPED POTS

Hide plastic flowerpots inside larger plastic pots, swathed in fabric to coordinate cleverly with your chosen furnishings.

MATERIALS

Light to mediumweight fabric

PVA adhesive

Measuring jug

Old mixing bowl

Old spoon

Rubber gloves

Plastic flowerpot

Pencil and ruler

Tape measure

Drawing pins

1 **CUTTING THE FABRIC**
You'll need sufficient fabric to create a generous swathed effect, so measure the depth of the flowerpot, double this and add 8cm (3¼in) for turnings. Then measure around the rim and add half that measurement again to allow for the front overlap. Cut out a rectangle of fabric to these measurements.

2 **MIXING THE ADHESIVE**
With an old spoon, mix one teacup of water and four of adhesive in the plastic bowl. Stir the mixture well.

3 **PREPARING THE FABRIC**
Press a 1cm (⅜in) turning to the wrong side along one long edge of the fabric. This edge will go along the bottom of the pot, so take care with the direction of the fabric pattern. Immerse the fabric in the adhesive and smooth off the excess. Rinse out the bowl in water.

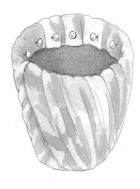

4 **WRAPPING THE FLOWERPOT**
Place the pressed-back edge of the fabric diagonally over the pot, starting just under the rim, and pleat the short end evenly. Wrap the fabric round the pot, scrunching it up as you go.

5 **FINISHING WRAPPING**
Pleat the opposite short edge and fold the excess fabric over the rim. Smooth the pleats to the inside. Trim the excess fabric inside the pot to within 5cm (2in) of the rim.

6 **SECURING THE EDGE**
To hold the pleats in place while the fabric dries, push drawing pins into the fabric on the inside, taking care not to crack the plastic.

7 **FINISHING OFF THE BASE**
Turn the pot over. Fold and pleat the fabric flat against the pot base and secure it with drawing pins. Leave the finished pot to dry in a warm room on top of a radiator or balanced on a clothes airer. Check the pleats regularly to make sure they stay in place, and adjust them if necessary.

◀ **Make a fabric-wrapped pot to enhance the colour scheme of your room. To complete the coordinated effect, choose a plant which echoes the colours of the fabric, such as this pretty pink busy lizzie.**

Formal Style Dining Room

If you have a separate dining room it can be fun on a special occasion to turn it into a miniature banqueting hall for a party. Use shimmering fabrics to dress up chairs, make sparkling table accessories and dress curtains with luxurious gold trimmings.

In this room you can make:
- Quick seat covers
- Flower posy trims
- Draped curtain pole
- Gilt-edged glassware

Tie flower posies set in a fabric ruffle onto your chairbacks for decoration.

Create a star-spangled gift with net, stars and curled ribbons.

Make folded water lily napkins and ivy leaf place cards.

CELEBRATING IN STYLE

A really special occasion, such as a wedding anniversary or an important family birthday, calls for a celebratory flourish. Use the existing colour scheme in your dining room as a starting point, and then add a dramatic sparkle with a few clever, quick and inexpensive effects.

In this formal style dining room, warm yellow walls, mellow toned furniture and a rich, green carpet have been spiced up with layered shimmering gold and green fabrics, gold stars and glitter, lush foliage and flower posies and sparkling, gilt-edged glassware. The transformation is focused on the dining table and chairs, but the draped window has also been given a decorative flourish with silky cords and glittery gold chains to elegantly complete the look.

Any colour scheme can be dressed up in this way. Enhance a fresh blue and cream dining room with shimmering silver trimmings; you could drape the window with silver beaded strings, use silvery blue shot organza over silver lamé for the chair seat covers, and white and blue flowers teamed with silvery grey foliage for the posies. For a vibrant effect, spice up a red-based scheme with glowing bronze details in a similar fashion.

QUICK SEAT COVERS

These drop-in seat covers are quick to make and will give your dining chairs an instant new look. Make them from two layers of fabric – a sheer fabric, such as chiffon or organza, laid over gold lamé or another gleaming metallic cloth, which will shine through. Alternatively, use a single layer of heavier shimmering fabric, such as a heavyweight shot taffeta.

MATERIALS

Metallic fabric

Sheer fabric

Narrow tape or cord

Matching sewing thread

Tape measure

Dressmakers' marker pen

Scissors

Pins

Bodkin or large safety pin

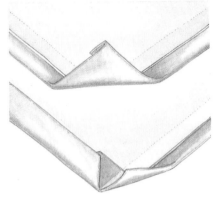

1 CUTTING THE COVERS
Lay the two fabrics out together, wrong side up, with the sheer fabric underneath the metallic one. Pin them together around the edges. Remove the chair seat from the chair by pushing it up from underneath, and lay it on the fabric as a pattern. Draw around the chair seat, adding a 10cm (4in) border all round. Cut out the piece and use it as a pattern for the other chairs.

2 MAKING THE COVERS
Press a 1cm (⅜in) then a 2cm (¾in) hem to the wrong side all round the fabric pieces, mitring the corners as shown. Stitch the hem in place, close to the inner edge, leaving a 5cm (2in) opening at the back of the seat. Thread the bodkin or safety pin with a piece of cord or tape, long enough to go all round the hem plus 20cm (8in) for the ties, and thread it through the channel.

◄ **Gold and green shot organza has been laid over lightweight gold lamé to create this quick chair seat cover. The same organza has been used to create the flower posy frill.**

3 FITTING THE COVERS
Lay the cover over the chair seat, with the sheer fabric uppermost. Pull on the cords or tapes to gather up the cover to fit the seat. Tie the cord or tape ends together securely, then put the seat back into the chair frame. Repeat steps 2-3 to make up the other chair covers.

CHAIRBACK POSIES

Complete the transformation of your dining chairs by making these pretty posies that fit neatly on the back of each dining chair. They make an original way of presenting a floral decoration. Mix fresh and silk flowers in toning colours, and then surround the blooms with a pretty soft ruffle in the same fabrics you used for the chair seat cover.

MATERIALS

For each posy

40cm (½yd) of metallic fabric

40cm (½yd) of sheer fabric

Matching sewing thread

About 60cm (24in) of 2.5cm (1in) wide elastic

Selection of fresh and silk flowers and foliage

Florists' binding wire

Florists' green gutta-percha tape

Two hook and loop fastenings

Large safety pin

Scissors

Tape measure

1 PREPARING THE FABRICS
Lay the two fabrics out together, wrong side up, with the sheer fabric underneath the metallic one. Pin them together. Cut out a 70 x 20cm (28 x 8in) piece. Press a 1cm (⅜in) hem along both long edges. Bring the short ends together, stitch and press the seam open.

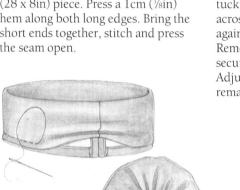

2 FORMING THE RUFFLE
With the wrong sides together, fold the fabric over to bring the two hemmed edges together. Run a gathering thread along the hemmed edges through all thicknesses. Pull on the threads to gather up the fabric, leaving a hole about 2.5cm (1in) across in the middle to allow for the flower stems.

3 MAKING THE STRAPS
Cut two lengths of elastic to fit snugly round the top bar of the chair back. From your layers of fabric, cut two 7cm (2¾in) wide strips twice the length of the elastic. Press a 5mm (¼in) hem to the wrong side on both long edges of the strips. Fold each strip in half, wrong sides together, and stitch close to the edge along both long edges.

4 INSERTING THE ELASTIC
Pin a large safety pin on to one end of a length of elastic, to stop it disappearing into the fabric tube. Thread the other end of the elastic through the tube, ruching the fabric over it. When you reach the other end, tuck in the raw fabric ends and stitch across through all layers; stitch across again 1cm (⅜in) in from the end. Remove the safety pin, then neaten and secure the other end in the same way. Adjust the ruffles. Repeat on the remaining strap.

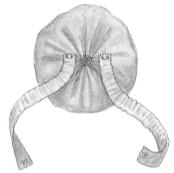

5 SECURING THE STRAPS
On each strap, stitch a fastening hook just inside one end. Stitch the loops to the other ends, on the other side of the straps. Oversew the loop end of each strap on to the ruffle, with the loops exposed, placing one strap on each side of the hole.

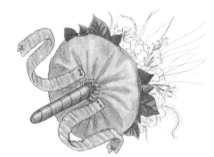

6 ADDING THE FLOWERS
Cut the silk and fresh flower stems to about 7.5cm (3in). Wire the stems of the fresh flowers if necessary. Bind the stems together with wire, and wind them with florists' tape. Push the stems through the hole in the ruffle.

GILDED GLASSWARE

Add shimmering gold detailing to glass plates for a truly festive look. The bobble-edged plates featured here have had tiny gold stars scattered round the rims, and their bobbled edges coloured with gold felt-tip pen. All the detailing is easily removable – just wipe off the felt-tip pen with lighter fuel and brush off the stars. Use the plates as decorative underplates to enhance your dinner service.

You can buy plain and coloured bobble-edged plates from some glassware and kitchenware stockists.

MATERIALS

Bobble-edged glass plates

Gold felt-tip pen

Tiny gold foil stars

Fine watercolour brush

Jar of water

Clean cloth

Newspaper to cover work surface

Lighter fuel

BEADED EDGING *Tip*

You can give cheap glass plates a gold bobbled edge by simply sticking on gold or bronze beads at 1.5cm (⅝in) intervals, using instant bonding adhesive.

▼ Gilded detailing gives these glass plates an extra sparkle. None of the detailing is permanent – the gold ink can be wiped off with lighter fuel and the stars simply brush off.

1 GILDING THE BOBBLES
Using the felt-tip pen, colour in the gold bobbles around the edges of the plates, colouring in all the bobbles on some plates, and alternate bobbles on others (make sure there is an even number of bobbles if you're colouring in alternate ones). Use a cloth moistened with lighter fuel to clean up any smudges. Leave the ink to dry thoroughly before use.

2 ADDING THE STARS
Using the watercolour brush, apply a little water round the outer rim of a plate. Sprinkle the tiny stars at random over the dampened area. Press them down lightly with the brush. On another plate, apply water in a swirl across the plate and sprinkle on a 'Milky Way' of stars. Repeat to decorate all the plates with stars in this way.

▶ Add a flourish to a special gift with a flamboyant wrapping, using tissue paper, net, foil stars and giftwrap ribbon. Place the gift in a square box, and wrap it in bright tissue paper – green was used here. Cut two large squares of net in different toning shades, like these dark and pale greens, and lay one over the other. Centre the box over the net and pull up the edges all round, securing them with a rubber band. Cover the band with gold and yellow giftwrap ribbons, curling the ends with a scissor blade. Slip different sizes of gold stars into the net.

Formal Style Dining Room – Table settings

Add elegant finishing touches to your celebratory dining table with folded flower napkins and cut-out ivy-leaf place cards. Dress up a draped curtain pole with lengths of gold cord, matching tassels and strings of sparkling beads.

▼ Use simple origami folds to turn table napkins into graceful, petalled flowers, and create exquisite place cards with an ivy leaf design.

When you dress up your dining room for a really special occasion, the focus of the celebration will be the dining table. Elegantly folded napkins like these waterlily shapes, created using simple origami folds, lend an instant air of style and glamour to any table

setting. Coordinate crisp cotton or linen napkins with your dining room decor for a sophisticated feel.

Writing your guests' names on a plain folded card to show them to their seat will make them feel welcome, but it only takes a little extra

time to cut out these ivy shapes and add a fresh green ivy sprig.

Creating the total look includes the background. An opulent draped curtain pole, dripping with rich cords and beads, will really set the scene for a special celebration.

IVY PLACE CARDS

Make these attractive name cards to direct your guests to their places in style. The cut-out ivy leaves echo the tiny sprigs of real ivy slotted into each card, and touches of colour and sparkle are added with a touch of green paint and a gold felt tip pen.

MATERIALS

Stiff, textured paper, such as parchment or watercolour paper

Ruler and pencil

Green watercolour paint

Fine artists' brush

Fine gold felt-tip pen

Fountain pen and green ink

Fine craft knife and cutting mat

PLACE CARD TEMPLATE

fold line

cutting lines

cutting lines

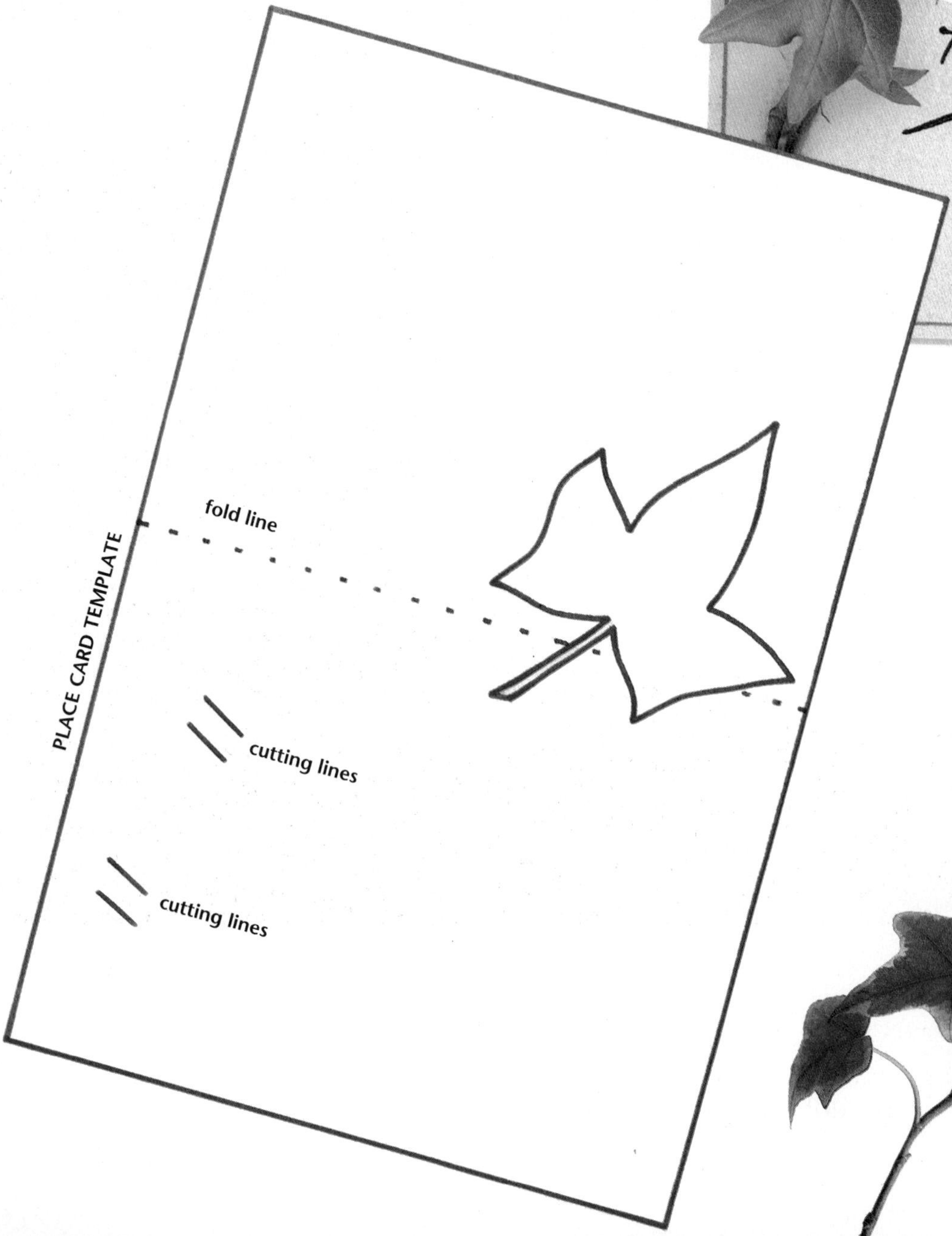

1 CUTTING OUT THE CARD Using the pencil and ruler, trace the template on to the paper, including the ivy leaf and the two sets of cutting lines at the bottom left. Using the craft knife and cutting mat, cut out the card around the edges.

2 CUTTING THE DESIGN

Fold the card in half widthways and press along the fold. Open it out again. Using the craft knife, carefully cut around the ivy leaf *above the fold line only*. Cut along the fold line to remove the small triangular section between the leaf and stem. Slit the cutting lines at the bottom left of the card.

3 ADDING THE COLOUR

Fold the card in half again and ease the leaf upright. Using the green watercolour paint and the fine brush, shade in the area just below the leaf to create the impression of a shadow cast over the card by the leaf.

4 EDGING WITH GOLD

Open out the card and lay it flat. Using the gold pen and ruler, draw a line along the sides and base of the *front* of the card only, 3mm (⅛in) in from the edge.

5 FINISHING OFF

Follow steps 1-4 to make the other cards. Using the fountain pen and green ink, write the names of your guests on the cards in a flowing script. Fold the cards in half again, and thread one or two sprigs of ivy through the slots at the left of each card.

▲ Dress up a draped curtain pole with lengths of gold furnishing cord, sparkling strings of beads and a few opulent gold tassels. You'll find beaded strings like the ones used here amongst the seasonal decorations in department stores, or you can use inexpensive bead necklaces instead.

Cut a double length of cord, about two and a half times the window width, sealing the ends with sticky tape. Starting at one end of the pole and using the picture as a guide, loop the cord around the pole; vary the depth of the loops and use pins to hold the cord in place. Pin the beaded strings in deep loops across the pole. Hang gold tassels from the finials to complete the effect.

FOLDED FLOWER NAPKINS

Use simple origami techniques to fold crisp cotton or linen napkins into multi-petalled flowers, which you can use to grace each place setting. For the best results, use quite large, square napkins which will make soft, full flowers.

1 FOLDING IN THE CORNERS
Press the napkin well and lay it flat on the table, with the wrong side up. Fold each corner into the centre to make a smaller square.

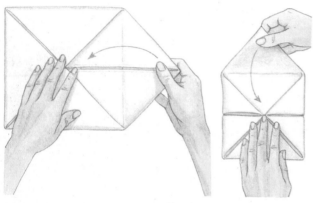

2 FOLDING THE CORNERS AGAIN
Fold the corners into the centre of the napkin a second time, creating an even smaller square. Turn the folded napkin over, and fold the corners in a third time, to make a smaller square; use your fingers to hold the folds down at the centre of the napkin as you work.

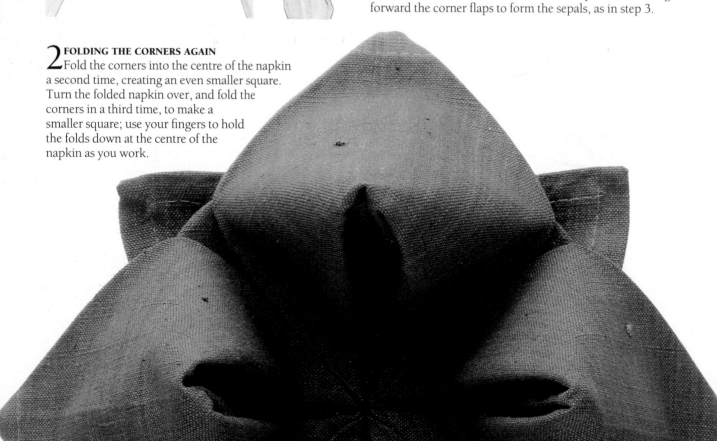

3 FORMING THE PETALS
Holding the centre folds in place with one hand, put your other hand behind the napkin and carefully draw one of the corners from the centre back outwards until it forms a peak, cupping the folded corner. Repeat at each corner to form four 'petals'.

4 FORMING THE SEPALS
Reach behind the flower, between the petals, and bring forward the corner flaps to form the sepals, as in step 3.

Colour Theme Dining Room

For a totally different look, try these crisp colours – ideal for a kitchen-diner. Green and white give a fresh look. Adorn your table with lavish green and white table linen and your chairs with plump and inviting frilled cushions.

In this room you can make:
- Director's chair covers
- Frilled and bordered cushion covers
- Frilled tablecloth
- Set of decorated glasses

◄ Make a pretty frilled cushion cover and a coordinating tie-on cover from striped and plain cotton fabrics.

► Decorate glasses and a water jug with painted stripes, and sew frilled napkins and appliqué placemats to complete the summer table setting.

GREEN AND WHITE SCHEME

A deep, vivid green that echoes the natural green of plants combines with white to form a vibrant backdrop for summer lunches or informal suppers with an al fresco feel. The scheme works by mixing a green and white striped fabric, plain green and plain white fabrics in different combinations to create a complete range of furnishings and accessories from chair covers to napkins and cutlery ties.

These colours work particularly well in a room with an outdoor focus, such as French windows leading on to a patio, where the natural green of the fabric forms a direct colour link with the foliage outside.

Offset your green and white soft furnishings with neutral floorboards, white muslin curtains and large, leafy indoor plants.

RE-COVERING A DIRECTOR'S CHAIR

Give old director's chairs a new lease of life with fresh green and white covers. Use deckchair canvas or a similar, strong fabric which will wear well.

Different chairs are constructed in different ways, so always check how the old cover is attached and secure the new cover in the same way. These instructions are for a director's chair with a tilting back.

MATERIALS

1m (1⅛yd) of green and white striped deckchair canvas

Calico or paper to make a pattern

Hammer and tacks or a staple gun and staples

Old screwdriver

Heavy-duty sewing machine needle

Heavy-duty sewing thread

Large eyelet kit

Pencil

1 REMOVING THE OLD COVERS
Turn the chair upside down and, using a pencil, mark the edge of the seat fabric on the wooden side bars to show where the new cover should go. Prise out the old tacks and staples with the screwdriver. Carefully remove back and seat covers, noting how everything is attached and in what order washers and bolts fit back together.

2 CUTTING OUT THE SEAT AND BACK
Pin the old seat cover to a piece of calico or a large sheet of paper. Draw round it, adding 2cm (¾in) on each long edge for a double hem, or 1cm (⅜in) if you are using a selvedge. Add 1cm (⅜in) on each short edge for turnings. Cut out the pattern and use it to cut out the canvas. Make a pattern for the chair back and cut it out in the same way.

3 HEMMING THE SEAT
Using the heavy-duty needle and strong thread, stitch a double 1cm (⅜in) hem on each long edge. Run a second row of stitching close to the first. Turn 1cm (⅜in) to the wrong side along each short edge. Prepare the chair back in the same way.

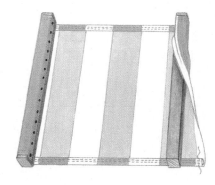

4 ATTACHING THE SEAT
Lay the chair on its side and place one folded edge of fabric along the pencil line marked on the side bar. Staple or hammer a tack through the fabric, close to the folded edge, into the centre of the bar. Staple or hammer tacks in all the way along the bar, spacing them out evenly so that the outer tacks lie close to the corners of the fabric. Fix the other end of the seat cover to the other side bar in the same way.

5 MARKING THE EYELET POSITIONS
Wrap the canvas round one side of the chair back. The fabric will wrap around the side bar, so the bolt will go through the fabric on each side of the bar. Mark the bolt positions.

6 INSERTING THE EYELETS
Remove the fabric. Following the manufacturer's instructions, insert a large eyelet at each bolt position.

Repeat steps 5 and 6 to mark and insert eyelets on the other side of the chair, making sure the fabric fits snugly across the chair back.

7 ATTACHING THE BACK
Place the outer eyelet over the bolt hole on one side of the chair and then staple or hammer a tack through the middle of the hem into the bar, level with the eyelet. Starting in the centre, tack or staple along the rest of the hem, placing the last tack just inside the edge of the fabric. Repeat for the other side of the chair back.

8 FINISHING THE BACK
Roll the fabric round the bar until the inner eyelet lines up with the other side of the bolt hole. Place the bolt through the eyelets and bar. Fix the chair back in position on the seat with wing nuts and washers.

FRILLED CUSHION

Enhance the comfort of your director's chair with this frilled cushion.

MATERIALS

40cm (16in) square cushion pad

50cm (½yd) of 120cm (45in) wide green furnishing fabric

20cm (8in) of 120cm (45in) wide green and white striped fabric

28cm (11in) zip

Matching cotton thread

CUTTING LIST

From green fabric
- One 43cm (17¼in) square
- Two 43cm x 23cm (17¼ x 9¼in) rectangles

From striped fabric
- Two 120 x 10cm (45 x 4in) strips

Note: take 1.5cm (⅝in) seams throughout.

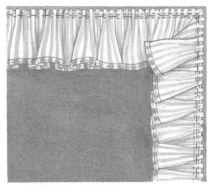

1 SEWING THE FRILL
With the right sides together, join the ends of the two fabric strips to make a circle. Turn up a 1cm (⅜in) double hem along the lower long edge and machine stitch it.

Mark the frill into four equal sections. Between each mark, stitch two rows of gathering threads on each side of the stitching line, 1.5cm (⅝in) in from the long raw edge.

2 ATTACHING THE FRILL
With the right sides together, and raw edges matching, pin the frill to the fabric square with the marks at the corners. If necessary, snip into the frill at the corners for ease. Pull up the gathering threads to fit, allowing a little extra fullness at the corners. Tack the frill in place.

3 MAKING THE CUSHION BACK
With right sides facing, pin the two fabric rectangles together. Machine stitch one long edge for 7.5cm (3⅛in) at each end, leaving a 28cm (11in) opening for the zip.

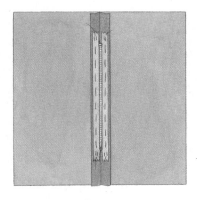

4 INSERTING THE ZIP
Press the seam open. Place the zip face down over the wrong side of the seam opening and tack it in place. With the right side of the fabric up, machine stitch the zip close to the teeth. Open the zip.

5 FINISHING THE CUSHION COVER
With the right sides together, place the back cover on top of the front cover, sandwiching the frill in between. Stitch around all four edges of the cover. Remove the tacking. Turn the cover out through the zip.

BORDERED CUSHION

This bordered cushion has tie fastenings instead of a zip. With a design feature like this, you can mix and match fabrics, making the ties from a contrast or coordinating print. Here, a small-scale stripe teams with the bolder stripe used for the centre panel.

MATERIALS

40cm (16in) square cushion pad

50cm (½yd) of 120cm (45in) wide green furnishing fabric

30cm (⅜yd) of 120cm (45in) wide striped green and white fabric

Matching cotton thread

CUTTING LIST

From green fabric
- Two 43cm (17¼in) squares

From green and white striped fabric
- One 30cm (12in) square
- Six 15 x 7cm (6 x 2¾in) strips of striped fabric

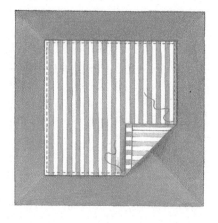

1 STITCHING THE FRONT PANEL
Fold one green fabric square in half diagonally and press it. Open out the square and repeat along the other diagonal. On the striped square, press under 1.5cm (⅝in) on each edge.

With the right sides up, pin the striped square centrally on to the green fabric square, using the diagonal foldlines as a guide. Topstitch it in place, close to the edges. Press the fabric to remove the foldlines.

2 STITCHING THE COVER
With the right sides facing, pin the two large squares together. Taking 1.5cm (⅝in) seams, stitch them round three sides. On the fourth side, stitch 5cm (2in) at each end, leaving a central gap. Round the gap, turn under 5mm (¼in), then 1cm (⅜in) to make a hem, and slipstitch it. Turn the cover out.

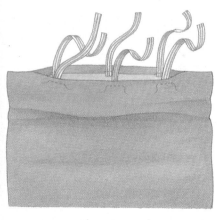

3 MAKING THE TIES
Fold each fabric strip in half lengthways with the right sides together and stitch along one long edge and one end. Turn it out and press it. Tuck the raw edges inside and slipstitch the opening closed. Space the ties across the open edge of the cushion, placing three ties on each side. Topstitch them in place. Insert the cushion pad and knot the ties.

▲ The frilled side panels of this stylish fitted tablecloth echo the design details on the cushions and table napkins. To make the tablecloth, join fabric widths to make a piece 1½ times the measurement round the table. For a frill with a mid-length drop, divide the table height by two and add 3cm (1¼in) for the hem. Join the fabric widths with French seams. Then gather up the frill to fit a top fabric panel.

Colour Theme Dining Room – Matching napkins

Colourful green and white striped table linen will transform your dining table for special family meals or dinner parties. Make frilled napkins and scalloped placemats, and paint a clear glass jug and glasses to match.

▼ Make a set of crisp white cotton napkins trimmed with green and white striped frills and decorated with novel vegetable appliqué motifs.

Green and white accessories will give your dining table all the freshness of summer, whatever the season. Make some accessories yourself, and buy a few extra items, like green cutlery, to complete the look.

Frilled napkins are easy to sew, and you can make coordinating placemats with striking scalloped borders. Paint a plain glass jug and tumblers with coordinating green stripes and a paler leaf motif for the final touch.

PEPPER TEMPLATE

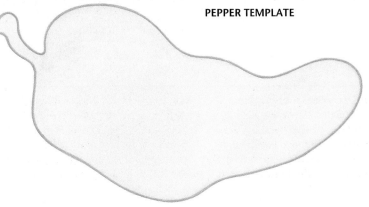

APPLIQUE NAPKINS

Make a set of frilled napkins decorated with vegetable appliqués. The appliqué shapes are made from a fine, washable craft felt, which you can buy from department stores and haberdashery shops. For the main napkin square, use a mediumweight cotton fabric.

The materials listed below will make a set of six napkins. Each finished napkin is 50cm (20in) square.

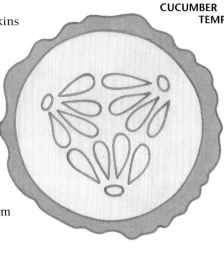

CUCUMBER TEMPLATE

PARSLEY TEMPLATE

MATERIALS

1.3m (1½yd) of 90cm (36in) wide plain white fabric

1m (1⅛yd) of 120cm (1⅜yd) wide green and white striped fabric

10.1m (11yd) of green bias binding

Two 23cm (9in) squares of pale green craft felt, such as Funtex

20cm (8in) square of stiff card

Fusible webbing (Bondaweb)

Dark green fabric pen

Sharp scissors

Tracing paper and pencil

CUTTING LIST

From white fabric
● Six 42cm (16½in) squares
From striped fabric
● Twelve 7.5cm (3in) deep strips, cut across the full fabric width
Note: take 1cm (⅜in) seams throughout unless otherwise stated.

1 MAKING THE FRILL
Using French seams, stitch the short edges of two strips of green and white striped fabric together to make a ring. Machine stitch a 6mm (¼in) double hem on one long edge.

2 ATTACHING THE FRILL
Mark the frill into four equal sections and work two rows of running stitch between the marks. Placing one mark at each corner of a white square, gather up the frill evenly and tack it around the square. Stitch it in place.

3 NEATENING THE RAW EDGES
Cut an 168cm (66in) length of bias binding. Lay the napkin flat with the wrong side of the frill facing upwards, and pin the opened bias binding, with the right side down, over the frill stitching line. Stitch it in place along the binding crease. Lay the napkin flat and press the bias binding up towards the centre of the napkin to enclose the raw edges of the frill. Pin and stitch the binding in place.

4 PREPARING THE MOTIFS
Trace the three vegetable motifs (see above and previous page) on to a piece of stiff card and cut them out.

Following the manufacturer's instructions, iron a piece of fusible webbing on to one side of the pale green craft felt. Place the templates on to the fusible webbing side of the craft felt, draw round them with a pencil and cut them out. If you are making six napkins, cut out two of each vegetable shape.

5 APPLYING THE MOTIFS
Peel the paper backing from one motif and position it on one corner of the napkin. Cover it with a clean cloth and iron it in place. To make sure the motif doesn't come off in the wash, use a matching thread to zigzag stitch around the edges.

For the cucumber motif, use the template, above, as a guide to draw in the seeds and skin with the dark green fabric pen.

PLACEMATS

These placemats are made from the same striped fabric as the napkin frills, and have a plain border. The materials given below are for six placemats.

Each finished placemat measures 45 x 30cm (17¾ x 12in).

MATERIALS

2m (2⅛yd) of 120cm (48in) wide green and white striped fabric

1m (1⅛yd) of 120cm (48in) wide plain green fabric

Fusible webbing (Bondaweb)

47 x 4.5cm (18½ x 1¾in) strip of stiff card

Tailors' chalk

Scissors

Ruler

Pencil

CUTTING LIST

From striped fabric
● Twelve 47 x 32cm (18½ x 12½in) rectangles

From plain green fabric
● Six 47 x 32cm (18½ x 12½in) rectangles

From fusible webbing
● Twelve 47 x 5cm (18½ x 2in) strips
● Twelve 22 x 5cm (8¾ x 2in) strips

Note: take 1.5cm (⅝in) seams, unless otherwise stated.

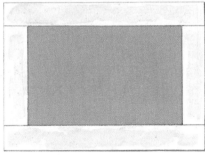

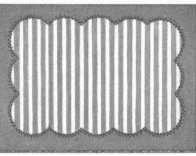

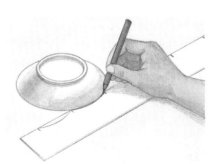

1 MAKING A BORDER TEMPLATE
Using the ruler and a pencil, make a mark 4.5cm (1¾in) in from each end of the card strip. Then mark the middle section into five equal parts of about 7.5cm (3in). Using a cup or saucer to draw around, join the pencil marks with a curve to create five scallops. Cut out the scalloped edge.

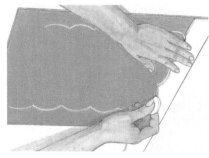

2 PREPARING THE FABRIC
On the wrong side of one green fabric rectangle, fuse a long strip of fusible webbing to each long edge and a short strip to each short edge.

3 CUTTING THE BORDER
Lay the green fabric rectangle right side up. Line up the straight edge of the template against the long edge of the fabric. Using tailors' chalk, draw around the scalloped edge. Repeat for the second long edge. Place the template on one short edge so that the scallops link up around the border. Trace off three scallops. Repeat for the other short edge. Cut along the marked lines to create the border.

4 STITCHING THE BORDER
Peel off the backing paper from the fusible webbing and, with the edges matching, place the border, webbing side down, on to the right side of one striped fabric rectangle. Following the manufacturer's instructions, fuse it in place. Using matching green thread, machine zigzag stitch around the scalloped edge.

5 FINISHING THE MAT
With the edges matching and the right sides together, place another striped fabric rectangle on top of the first, enclosing the border. Stitch around the edges, taking a 1cm (⅜in) seam allowance and leaving a small opening in one side to turn through. Turn the napkin through to the right side and slipstitch the opening closed. Press the napkin.

Using matching thread, machine topstitch around the outer edges of the border to keep them flat.

PAINTED JUG AND GLASSES

You can buy special paints for painting glassware from art shops and graphic suppliers. It is important to treat painted glassware with care – remember that it is not dishwasher-safe. This type of glassware is best kept for decorative and occasional use.

MATERIALS

20cm (8in) glass jug

Small glasses

Low-tack masking tape, such as Magic Tape

Deep green and yellow glass paint

Sharp craft knife and cutting board

Metal ruler and saucer

Small artists' brush

1 PREPARING THE MASKING TAPE
Cut several strips of masking tape 10cm (4in) long and 1cm (⅜in) wide.

2 APPLYING THE MASKING TAPE
Wash and dry the jug and glasses thoroughly to remove any grease or dust. Stick strips of tape vertically, 1cm (⅜in) apart, around the lower half of the jug and glasses. For the jug, cut off a 35cm (13¾in) length of tape and stick it around the jug 8cm (3¼in) from the base. For the glasses, cut 24cm (9½in) lengths of tape and stick them 6.5cm (2½in) from the base. Press down the tape edges firmly.

3 PAINTING THE STRIPES
Using the deep green glass paint, fill in the areas between the masking tape strips. Wait until the paint is completely dry (at least an hour) and then peel away the tape.

4 PAINTING THE LEAVES
In the saucer, mix a little green and yellow paint to make light green. Using the artists' brush, hand paint green leaves on to the top half of the jug.

5 FIXING THE PAINTS
Some glass paints need to be oven baked to fix them. Put the jug and glasses on to a baking tray and bake them following the manufacturer's instructions. Leave them to cool in the oven before removing them, otherwise they may crack or even shatter.

Scandinavian Style Kitchen

If you are lucky enough to have a large kitchen you'll soon find it will become a gathering place for your family. This Scandinavian style kitchen reflects traditional European folk art schemes where practicality and comfort are a must.

In this room you can make:
- Appliquéd tea towels and place mats
- A welcoming wreath
- Decorative hooks for kitchen accessories

For a homely feel make a wreath of padded hearts.

Add flair to breakfast with appliquéd place mats.

Go for a rustic look with fabric-decorated boxes.

Work an embroidery with a happy message.

SCANDINAVIAN KITCHEN

This Scandinavian style kitchen combines pale and muted colours with pretty fabrics and traditional folk motifs to create a calm and welcoming atmosphere. The look is perfect for kitchens where you want a room which is practical and comfortable.

To copy this look, choose a natural floor surface, such as stripped and varnished wood, or terracotta tiles.

Paint the walls white, and choose two soft shades of green for the cupboards and drawer units, using the lighter colour to highlight the panelling.

Add a medley of pretty accessories, made from toning fabrics, such as a pan-holder, tea towels and place mats decorated with appliquéd hearts. Continue the theme by stencilling kitchen equipment to match.

HEART WREATH

Welcome visitors to your kitchen with this delightful heart wreath. It's made of mini fabric hearts sewn on to a heart-shaped wire frame. You can buy the type of strong wire you need for this project at hardware and DIY stores. The finished wreath is about 40cm (16in) across.

MATERIALS

Remnants of ten different blue, green and white mini-print cotton fabrics

2m (2¼yd) of 4cm (1½in) wide double-sided blue satin ribbon

Mediumweight wadding

Matching threads

Strong buttonhole thread

Tracing paper

Stiff paper or card

Paper and pencil

Scissors

1.40m (1⅝yd) of strong wire

Wire clippers

Piece of wood or board about 40cm (16in) square

Small nails

Hammer

Coarse file (optional)

HEART PATTERN

CUTTING LIST

Trace the heart pattern on to stiff paper or card to make a template. Use this template to cut out the hearts.
From each of the ten fabrics
● 10 hearts (100 hearts in total)
Note: take 1cm (⅜in) seam allowances

1 ASSEMBLING THE HEARTS
Pin two hearts in the same fabric right sides together, and stitch all round, leaving a small gap to turn out. Trim the seams and clip the curves for ease. Turn the heart out to the right side and fill it with bits of wadding. Oversew the gap closed. Make 50 hearts in this way (five in each fabric).

2 PREPARING THE WOOD
Enlarge the heart motif so that it is about 35cm (13¾in) high. Cut it out to make a template. Lay the template on the piece of wood and draw round it with a pencil. Hammer the nails into the wood at regular intervals along the drawn outline.

◄ This welcoming heart wreath is made from padded fabric hearts, densely packed on to a heart-shaped wire frame and stitched in place. A combination of blue, green and white mini-print fabrics is used for the hearts so that they coordinate with the soft colours of the kitchen.

3 SHAPING THE WIRE FRAME
Push the centre of the wire into the dip at the top centre of the heart, then carefully bend the wire around the outside of the remaining nails. Twist the ends together at the base, and trim them, using the wire clippers. Remove the nails, as necessary, then lift the heart frame off the board.

4 SEWING ON THE HEARTS
If you like, rub over the frame with the coarse file to roughen the surface – this will make it easier to attach the hearts. Using the buttonhole thread, oversew the hearts on to the frame one by one. Cover the frame completely, alternating the colours of the hearts and using the picture above as a guide.

5 ADDING THE RIBBON BOW
Fold the ribbon in half to find the centre. Holding the centre at the top of the heart wreath, wrap one half loosely around the right side of the wreath and the other half around the left side of the wreath. Tie the ends in a neat bow at the base of the heart. Trim the ribbon ends at an angle.

STENCILLED POT

Make this holder for your kitchen utensils – it's a terracotta pot, decorated with a stencilled heart and leaf motif to coordinate with the Scandinavian kitchen. This pot is unglazed, so it's easy to stencil with acrylic paints. If you have a glazed pot, you can still decorate it, but you must use special ceramic paint. A stencil brush was used to paint the design in the picture, but you could use a natural sponge if you want a softer effect.

MATERIALS

Large terracotta pot

Acrylic paints for unglazed terracotta, or ceramic paints for glazed terracotta, in blue, grey-blue and blue-green

Tracing paper and pencil

20 x 14cm (8 x 5½in) rectangle of card

Craft knife and cutting mat

Masking tape and pencil

Stencil brush or natural sponge

Old saucers for mixing the paint

1 CUTTING THE STENCIL
Trace off the stencil design (below left) and transfer it on to the card. Using the craft knife and cutting board, cut out the marked shapes.

STENCIL PATTERN

2 STENCILLING THE DESIGN
Using masking tape, fix the stencil on to the side of the pot. If you are using acrylic paints, dilute the three paint colours with a little water in the old bowls or saucers. If you are using ceramic paints, put a little of each colour into a separate bowl or saucer. Using the stencil brush or the natural sponge, apply the paint through the stencil – use grey-blue for the central heart, blue-green for the small, top heart and the ribbon at the base, and blue for the leaf shapes. Leave the paint to dry, then remove the stencil.

Scandinavian Style Kitchen – Place settings

Entice guests or the family to breakfast in your Scandinavian style kitchen with a pretty set of heart appliquéd place mats and coordinating heart-shaped napkins. You can also paint wooden accessories to match.

▼ **Make these pretty accessories for the breakfast table – there's a quilted and appliquéd place mat and an unusual heart-shaped napkin.**

HEART BREAKFAST MAT

The appliquéd heart motifs on this breakfast mat continue the traditional folk motif theme. Make the place mat from blue, cream and soft green fabrics to match the muted colour scheme of the room. If you like, you could use tea towels in a suitable fabric as the main fabric for the mat.

The place mat in the picture was quilted by hand but, for speed, you could machine quilt it. The finished place mat measures about 42 x 30cm (16½ x 12in).

MATERIALS

For each place mat

Two 42 x 30cm (16½ x 12in) rectangles of blue and white gingham fabric

28cm (11in) square of cream cotton fabric or calico

50cm (½yd) of 110cm (44in) wide green and white mini-print cotton fabric

Matching threads

Strong white sewing thread

42 x 30cm (16½ x 12in) rectangle of mediumweight wadding

Dressmakers' marker pencil

Tracing paper and card

Ruler

Sharp scissors and pins

CUTTING LIST

Trace the heart and leaf on to card and cut them out to make templates. Use these to cut out the following:

From cream cotton or calico
● Four hearts

From green and white fabric
● Six leaves
● Enough 4cm (1½in) wide bias strips joined together to make a strip 146cm (57½in) long

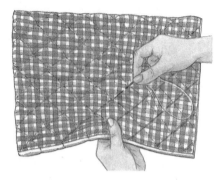

2 WORKING THE QUILTING
Pin the wadding between the two fabric rectangles, with the right sides facing out and the marked rectangle on the top. Starting at the centre, work small running stitches along each marked line, using the strong white sewing thread.

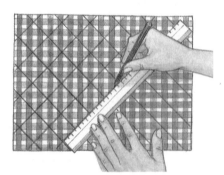

1 MARKING THE QUILTING LINES
Lay out one gingham rectangle, with the right side facing up. Using the ruler and dressmakers' marker pencil, mark a grid of diagonal lines 5cm (2in) apart on the fabric.

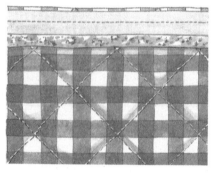

3 BINDING THE EDGES
Fold in the long edges of the bias strip by 1cm (⅜in), then fold it in half lengthways and press it. Use this to bind the raw edges of the mat, using the topstitched binding method and mitring the corners: take a 1cm (⅜in) seam allowance.

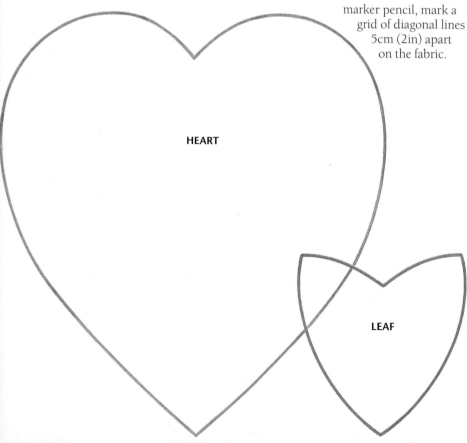

HEART

LEAF

4 PREPARING THE APPLIQUE
Stitch around each heart and leaf, just outside the 5mm (¼in) seam allowance. Cut notches in the curves up to the stitched lines for ease, and snip to the stitched lines at the top centre points.

HEART NAPKIN

When it's folded up, this ingenious napkin looks like a heart; when it's unfolded, it resembles a lucky four-leaved clover.

The finished napkin measures approximately 46cm (18in) square.

MATERIALS

For each napkin

100 x 50cm (40 x 20in) rectangle of green or blue and white mini-print cotton

Blue or green contrast sewing thread

Sharp scissors

Tracing paper and pattern paper

Tailors' chalk and pencil

NAPKIN PATTERN
One square = 2.5cm (1in)

5 PLACING THE APPLIQUE
Pin the hearts and leaves on to the place mat, spacing them evenly and using the picture as a guide. Oversew the shapes in place, tucking under the raw edges as you sew.

6 QUILTING THE HEARTS
Using the strong white sewing thread, work a line of running stitches around the cream hearts, close to the edges. Work the stitches through all the layers of fabric.

1 PREPARING THE PATTERN
Enlarge the heart pattern: each square on the grid represents 2.5cm (1in). Transfer it four times on to the pattern paper with the straight sides together, as shown left. Cut out the pattern along the outer, curved edge.

▶ Coordinate your breakfast table setting, both in colour and theme, with these crisp cotton napkins that fold into a heart shape. The napkins are generously sized and are made from two layers of fabric for added strength. Use the heart pattern given above to cut out as many as you need. All the stitching can be done on a sewing machine.

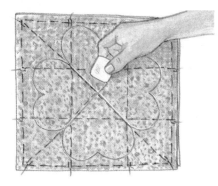

2 MARKING THE FABRIC

Fold the fabric in half widthways with the wrong sides together. Tack the layers together. Pin the pattern on to the fabric and chalk around it. Remove the pattern, then chalk in the straight lines between the hearts.

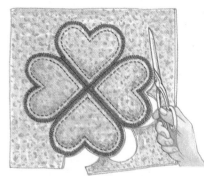

3 ZIGZAG STITCHING THE EDGES

Set the sewing machine to a close zigzag stitch. Using contrast sewing thread, zigzag stitch around each heart, working straight along one straight side, across the shaped top, and down the next straight side, and so on.

4 TOPSTITCHING THE NAPKIN

If you like, use the same sewing thread to work a line of topstitching around each heart just inside the zigzag stitching.

5 TRIMMING THE NAPKIN

Using sharp scissors, neatly trim the fabric close to the outer edge of the zigzag stitching. Remove the tacking stitches.

◀ This sturdy wooden trug is a practical and decorative accessory for the Scandinavian style kitchen. It has been painted in four different shades of blue to coordinate with the colours of the kitchen units and the stencilled pot. The inside (just seen) is painted a darker blue than the outside, the top edge a slightly paler blue, and the handle is painted strong blue for contrast.

The rough, painted texture contrasts perfectly with pots of fresh green herbs – basil, rosemary and parsley – and aromatic garlic bulbs.

Scandinavian Style Kitchen – Hooks & holders

Continue the folk motif theme in your Scandinavian style kitchen by bending wire into heart-shaped hooks. The hooks are easy to make and they're ideal for keeping kitchen essentials, like the delightful heart appliqué pot holder, close at hand.

▼ Twist wire to form these decorative heart-shaped hooks. Use them to hang tea towels or a practical pot holder, appliquéd with leaves and a heart.

KITCHEN HOOKS

It's surprisingly easy to make your own heart-shaped wire kitchen hooks, and they'll cost a fraction of the price of shop-bought ones. You'll need strong wire and fuse wire – you can buy these in hardware shops. The finished hooks are about 12cm (4¾in) high and 8cm (3¼in) across.

MATERIALS

For each hook:

60cm (24in) of wire 1.8mm in diameter

120cm (48in) of fuse wire

Wood offcut at least 17 x 12cm (7 x 4¾in)

Small nails

Hammer

Wire cutters or bolt cutters

Pliers

Tracing paper

Carbon paper

Pencil

Ruler

Thick protective gloves (optional)

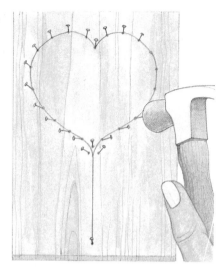

1 TRANSFERRING THE PATTERN
Trace off the heart hook pattern, including the dots. Using the carbon paper, transfer it on to the wood. Hammer small nails at an angle into the dots on the marked outline, so that they lean outwards slightly.

2 SHAPING ONE SIDE
If you like, wear thick gloves to protect your hands. Measure about 8cm (3¼in) from one end of the 1.8mm wire. Holding this point against the nail at the top centre of the heart shape, bend the wire carefully around the outside of the nails on the right side. When you reach the bottom of the heart shape, slip the wire *between* the last nail on the right side and the central one just above it.

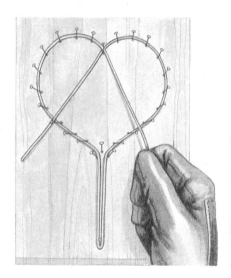

3 FINISHING THE HEART
Take the wire straight down to the nail below the heart and bend it round this nail, then back up again to the base of the heart shape.
Take the wire *between* the bottom nail on the left of the heart shape and the central nail just above it. Then bend the wire around the outside of the nails on the left of the heart shape, up to the top central nail. Lift the wire heart off the nails – remove the nails with pliers, if necessary.

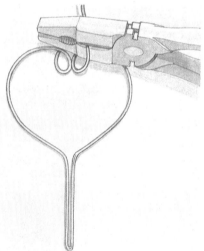

4 SHAPING THE LOOPS
Using the pliers, bend each end of the wire into a downward facing loop, then use the wire cutters to snip off the excess wire.

5 FIXING THE LOOPS
Bend the fuse wire in half. Wind it around the loops where they meet to bind them together securely. Then take one half of the fuse wire and bind it down the right half of the heart: bind the other half down the left half of the heart. When you reach the bottom, bind each end of the fuse wire around the tail of the thicker wire to hold it in place. Snip off any excess wire.

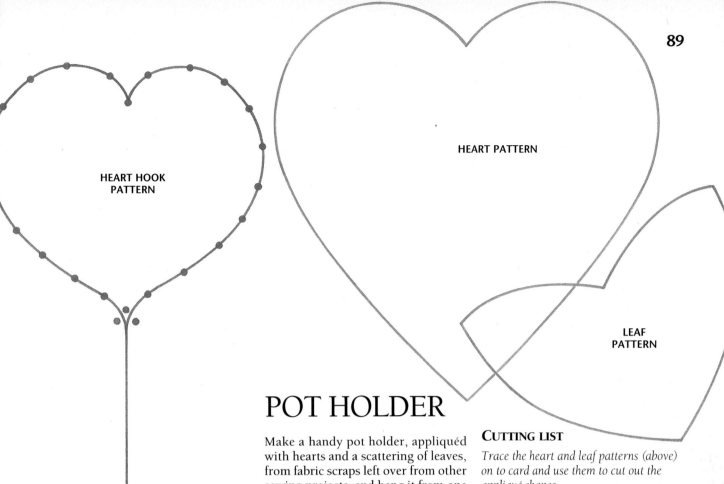

HEART HOOK PATTERN

HEART PATTERN

LEAF PATTERN

POT HOLDER

Make a handy pot holder, appliquéd with hearts and a scattering of leaves, from fabric scraps left over from other sewing projects, and hang it from one of your heart-shaped wire hooks.

The finished pot holder is about 22cm (8¾in) square.

MATERIALS

44 x 22cm (17½ x 8¾in) rectangle of cream cotton fabric or calico

30cm (12in) of 110cm (44in) wide dark blue mini-print cotton fabric for the binding

Scraps of green and light blue and white mini-print cotton fabrics for the appliqué

22cm (8¾in) square of heavyweight wadding

Matching sewing threads

Strong white thread for the quilting

Tracing paper

Card

Pencil

Adhesive

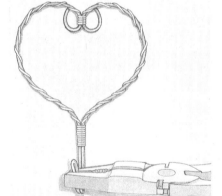

6 SHAPING THE HOOK
Using the pliers, bend up the lower half of the tail into a hook shape.

CUTTING LIST

Trace the heart and leaf patterns (above) on to card and use them to cut out the appliqué shapes.

From cream cotton or calico
- Two 22cm (8¾in) squares

From light blue mini-print fabric
- One heart

From green mini-print fabric
- Four leaf shapes
- One 10 x 2.5cm (4 x 1in) strip for the hanging loop

From dark blue mini-print fabric
- Enough 4cm (1½in) bias strips to make a strip 88cm (34¾in) long, allowing extra for joins

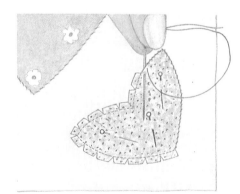

1 ADDING THE APPLIQUE SHAPES
Stitch around the light blue heart, 5mm (¼in) in from the edge. Clip the curves for ease up to the stitching line, and snip into the top of the heart. Pin the heart to the centre of one cream square. Oversew it in place, tucking under the raw edges as you sew. In the same way, appliqué a leaf shape about 4cm (1½in) from each corner, with the point facing towards the corner.

2 WORKING THE QUILTING
Pin the wadding between the appliquéd square and the plain cream cotton square, with the right sides facing out. Tack the layers together diagonally from corner to corner and across from the middle of the side edges. Using the strong white sewing thread, quilt a line of stitching 1cm (⅜in) inside the heart, then 1cm (⅜in) outside it. Remove the tacking.

3 MAKING THE HANGING LOOP
Fold the green strip of fabric in half lengthways with the right sides together and stitch 5mm (¼in) from the long raw edges. Turn the strip to the right side and press it. Fold it in half and pin it to one corner of the pot holder on the plain side, with the raw edges matching.

4 ADDING THE BINDING
Fold in the long edges of the bias strip by 1cm (⅜in) and press them in place. Fold the strip in half lengthways and press it again. Use this to bind the edges of the pot holder, mitring the corners neatly.

◀ Transform simple wooden boxes – these were cheese boxes – with paints and fabric ties to match your Scandinavian kitchen. Use the boxes to store bouquets garnis or spices, or simply to tidy kitchen clutter. Mix and match the paint and fabric colours; you can leave the box base plain, then paint the lid and rim in two shades, or you can paint the base and lid in a combination of shades.

Start by washing and drying the boxes to remove all traces of the previous contents, then select one, two or even three paint colours for each box (you can colour the inside too).

Make a fabric tie from a frayed length of cotton, and trim the ends with miniature padded hearts – you can make these by reducing one of the heart templates. Just stitch two fabric hearts together with the right sides facing, leaving a small gap to turn out. Turn out the heart, pad it with a little wadding and slipstitch the gap closed. Stitch a heart to each end of the tie.

Scandinavian Style Kitchen – Tapestry picture

Add pretty finishing touches to your Scandinavian style kitchen. Coordinate a tea towel with pretty appliqué designs, and give a plain kitchen apron a heart-shaped pocket. There's a traditional cross stitch picture with a warming message to work, as well.

▼ **This pretty cross stitch picture is worked in just three colours of embroidery cotton to echo the colours of the Scandinavian kitchen.**

APPLIQUED TEA TOWEL

This tea towel has been embellished with fabric appliqué to link it to the other kitchen accessories. If you like, you could make the tea towel from scratch, using a rectangle of strong, checked cotton or linen fabric. Cut the appliqué motifs from two pretty mini-print fabrics.

MATERIALS

Blue and white checked tea towel

40cm (½yd) of 110cm (44in) wide green mini-print cotton fabric

25cm (10in) square of light blue and white mini-print cotton fabric

White sewing thread

Tracing paper

Card

Adhesive

Pencil

CUTTING LIST

Enlarge the leaf and corner motif patterns on to card and cut them out to make templates. Use these to cut out the appliqué shapes.

From light blue and white fabric
- One corner motif with the heart shape cut out

From green mini-print fabric
- Two leaf motifs
- Enough 4cm (1½in) wide bias strips joined together to make a strip to fit round the tea towel, including extra for joins
- One 10 x 5cm (5 x 2in) strip for the hanging loop

1 PREPARING THE TEA TOWEL
Cut off the hems all round the tea towel. Lay out the tea towel, right side up. Pin the corner motif, right side up, to one corner. Trim the corner of the tea towel into a curve to match the motif. Pin a leaf motif about 2cm (¾in) from each indent on the corner motif.

2 STITCHING ON THE SHAPES
Oversew the leaves in place around the outside edges, tucking under the raw edges as you go. Oversew the corner motif in place around the inner curved edge only. Tack it along the outer edges. Using white sewing thread and a close machine zigzag, stitch around the raw edges of the cut-out heart (shown in blue for clarity).

3 FINISHING THE TEA TOWEL
Make the hanging loop and bind the edges of the tea towel, as for the POT HOLDER, steps 3-4.

▶ Appliqué mini print fabrics in heart and leaf shapes on to a checked blue and white tea towel. The motifs are sewn on to one corner of the tea towel, and the edge is bound with matching fabric.

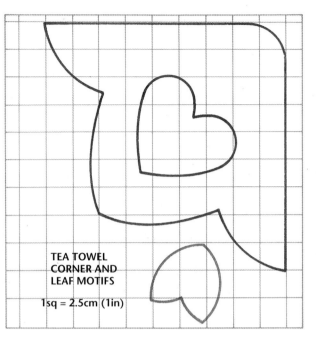

TEA TOWEL
CORNER AND
LEAF MOTIFS

1sq = 2.5cm (1in)

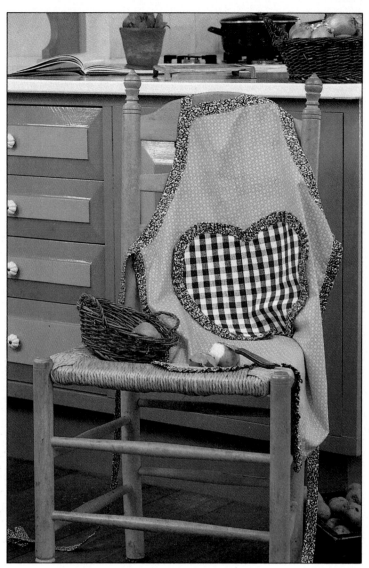

► To make the pocket on this apron, enlarge
one of the heart motifs on page 89 and cut it
out twice from fabric. For the frill, measure
around the heart, then cut a 7cm (2¾in) wide
strip of fabric twice this measurement. Stitch
the ends together with the right sides facing.
Fold the strip in half lengthways, right sides
out, press it, then gather it up and pin it to one
heart with the raw edges matching and the
right sides together. Stitch it in place. Stitch
the second heart on top with the right sides
facing, leaving a gap to turn out. Snip into the
seam allowances, turn out the heart and
slipstitch the gap closed. Topstitch the pocket
on the apron, leaving an opening at the top.

CROSS STITCH HEART PICTURE

Work this simple cross stitch picture
in threads to match your muted blue
and green kitchen colour scheme. The
finished picture measures approximately 32 x 30cm (12½ x 12in).

MATERIALS

42 x 40cm (16½ x 15¾in) piece of
ecru evenweave fabric with 11
threads per 2.5cm (1in)

DMC stranded embroidery cotton
in the colours specified in the key

Embroidery hoop

Tape measure

Frame

Thick card

Craft knife, metal ruler and cutting
board

◄This simple yet attractive cross
stitch picture would make a lovely
house-warming gift, so why not
stitch two?

1 WORKING THE EMBROIDERY
Mount the evenweave fabric in the
embroidery hoop. Starting with the
heart in the bottom right corner, work
the design in cross stitch, with the
point of the heart 8cm (3¼in) from the
edges. Use two strands of cotton and
work each cross stitch over two
threads, following the chart (overleaf)
for the colours.

2 FRAMING THE EMBROIDERY
Cover the embroidery with a cloth
and press it. Remove the backing
board from the frame and cut a piece of
thick card the same size, using the craft
knife and metal ruler. Lace the
embroidery over the card, then mount
it in the frame.

▼ Here is the chart for the pretty cross stitch picture. Work the embroidery in the colours shown in the key, using two strands of cotton and working each cross stitch over two fabric threads. If you like, you could make the picture for a different room setting, choosing embroidery cottons in three colours to match the main colours in the room. The finished picture measures 32 x 30cm (12½ x 12in).

KEY

■ green 993

■ dark blue 930

■ blue 794

Provençal Kitchen

If you just want to give your kitchen a new look, try this rustic French flavour by decorating it with colourful mix and match Provençal fabrics. Use them to make a patchwork cloth and to cover a mount for a cross stitch lavender picture.

▼ This patchwork tablecloth is simple to sew and can be adapted to any table size. It's made in the same fabrics as the frilled chair cushions.

▲ Embroider a delightful cross stitch lavender picture.

▲ Stencil a painted wooden tray and make quick jam pot covers.

▲ Make pretty, gathered shelf edgings for the kitchen.

CREATING THE LOOK

Bright Provençal prints, with their sunny colours and neat patterns, are perfect for kitchens. You can mix and match different Provençal prints, or introduce other patterns and plain fabrics in the same colours. Use the prints to make lots of pretty and useful items, such as the tablecloth and curtains, the quick-and-easy jam pot covers and fabric-wrapped baskets.

It's easy to mix prints in your kitchen, particularly when they're in toning colours. Choose two main colours as the basis of the scheme, such as the yellow and blue of this kitchen. Look at the swatches for other ideas – try blue and red or green and cream. Then choose two main Provençal prints based on your colour scheme, and add extra prints with similar colours but with motifs in different shapes and sizes.

Extend the theme by painting pieces of furniture and kitchen accessories, like chairs, a tray or an egg rack, in one of your main colours. You can then add further decoration to your painted items with a simple, graceful stencil which echoes the pretty designs on your fabrics.

PATCHWORK TABLECLOTH

This tablecloth combines three Provençal-style prints. Either copy the colours in the picture or choose your own colour scheme.

MATERIALS

Three printed fabrics

Matching sewing thread

Dressmakers' marker pen

Scissors

CUTTING LIST

Measure the length and width of the table and cut out the following:

From the main print (A)

● One piece the length of the table plus 25cm (10in) by the width of the table plus 25cm (10in) – if you need to join pieces, position the seams under the contrast bands, and allow extra fabric for the seams

From print B

● Four 30cm (12in) squares for the corner patches

From print C

● Two 8.5cm (3½in) wide strips the length of the large fabric rectangle
● Two 8.5cm (3½in) wide strips the width of the large fabric rectangle

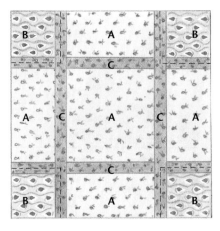

Note: cut the fabric along the straight grain and trim away the selvedges

▲ This egg rack has been painted blue to tie in with the yellow and blue Provençal kitchen.

1 ADDING THE CORNER SQUARES
Lay out the large rectangle with the right side up. Pin and tack a corner patch on to each corner with the raw edges matching.

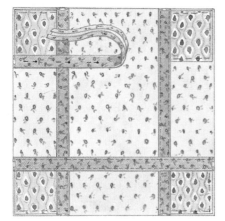

◄ Paint your accessories in one of the accent colours of your kitchen. Red is used in the fabrics in this kitchen, so this spoon holder has been varnished in deep red. It's used here to store fresh rosemary, it could also be used to hold wooden spoons.

2 ADDING THE BANDS
Press under 1cm (⅜in) along the long edges of each fabric strip. Using the diagram as a guide, pin the strips on to the large rectangle with the right sides facing up. Make sure the strips cover the edges of the corner patches. Stitch the strips in place, close to each edge. Press the cloth.

3 FINISHING THE TABLECLOTH
Turn a double 2.5cm (1in) hem all round the tablecloth, mitring the corners neatly. Machine stitch the hem in place.

► Green and cream fabrics work together to create a soft, fresh country look. For a varied effect, use a range of prints with motifs in different shapes and sizes.

LAVENDER PICTURE

This cross stitch picture has a pretty print mount that ties in with the Provençal theme.

MATERIALS

30cm (12in) square of evenweave embroidery fabric with 25 threads per 2.5cm (1in)

Embroidery cottons (see the key)

24cm (9½in) square of fabric

24cm (9½in) square of fusible webbing, such as Bondaweb

20cm (8in) square of lightweight wadding

Two 20cm (8in) squares of mounting card

Embroidery hoop

Multi-purpose glue

Craft knife and metal rule

Felt tip pen

20cm (8in) square picture frame

KEY		Anchor	DMC
◢	lilac	109	209
⊙	purple	111	552
⊟	pale lavender	117	341
⊠	lavender	118	340
⊡	light green	214	369
⊞	green	216	320

1 STITCHING THE EMBROIDERY
Mount the evenweave linen in the embroidery hoop. Following the chart, work the lavender design with two strands of embroidery cotton in cross stitch over two threads of fabric.

2 MAKING THE MOUNT
On one piece of mounting card, draw two diagonal lines from corner to corner to cross at the centre. Draw a 10cm (4in) window in the centre of the card, with its corners on the diagonal lines. Using the craft knife and rule, cut out the window and discard it.

3 PREPARING THE PIECES
Lay out the wadding, place the card mount on top and draw round it with a felt tip pen. Cut out the wadding.
   Iron the fusible webbing to the wrong side of the fabric square.

4 COVERING THE MOUNT
Glue the wadding to the card mount. Lay out the fabric, wrong side up, and peel off the backing. Place the mount, wadding side down, on top. Trim away the fabric allowance at the outer corners and snip to the mount at the inner corners, trimming away the excess fabric. Press the edges over the mount. Iron them to the back of the card, making sure the fabric lies smoothly over the wadded side.
   Lace the embroidery to the remaining card. Glue the mount on top, then remove the picture glass and slip the picture into the frame. Glue the backing from the frame to the back of the picture.

Provençal Kitchen – Café curtains

Decorate your Provençal kitchen with a set of bright café curtains and some pretty fabric accessories. To extend the colour scheme and the rustic French style to your kitchen furniture, there's also a simple stencil to use on a tray, chair or chest.

▼ **These simple café curtains are hung from pretty contrast ties. For a really coordinated look, the pole has been painted to match the ties.**

CAFE CURTAINS

Café curtains are a favourite for kitchens because they have an informal style and provide privacy without sacrificing light.

These curtains are easy to make. They're simple, unlined curtains, pleated and fastened on to a narrow, painted pole with contrasting bow ties.

MATERIALS

Print fabric for the curtains

Contrasting fabric for the ties

Matching sewing thread

Pencil

CUTTING LIST

Measure the window and cut out the following:

From main fabric
- Two lengths of fabric as long as the finished curtain plus 10cm (4in) and 1½-2 times the finished curtain width plus 10cm (4in).

From contrast fabric
- Sufficient 38 x 7.5cm (15 x 3in) strips to place at 10cm (4in) intervals across each curtain.

Note: if you need to join fabrics for the curtains, use French seams for neatness.

1 HEMMING THE EDGES
Turn under and pin a double 2.5cm (1in) hem on all the raw edges of each curtain rectangle, mitring the corners neatly. Stitch the hems neatly by machine or hand.

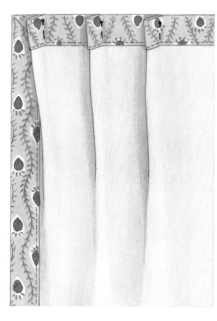

2 PLEATING THE TOP
At the top side edges of each curtain, fold and pin a 2cm (¾in) deep pleat. Make other pleats, spaced across the curtain at about 10cm (4in) intervals, and check that the pleated curtain is the correct width. Adjust the width of the pleats as necessary. Tack the pleats, then stitch them along the hem stitching line. Press each curtain.

3 MAKING THE TIES
Fold a fabric strip in half lengthways with the right sides together and stitch along one end and the long raw edge. Trim the seam allowances at the corners. Use the pencil to push the stitched end of the strip inside, to turn the strip right sides out. Press the tie flat, turn in the raw edges and slipstitch the opening closed. Repeat to make the other ties.

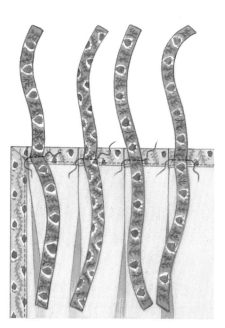

4 ATTACHING THE TIES
Lay out the curtain with the wrong side up. Fold each tie in half widthways and press it. Unfold the ties and pin one over each pleat on the curtain, with the fold just below the top of the curtain. Stitch each tie to the curtain along the foldline.

◄The chest and the chair show different decorative ways of using the same stencil designs. Below and overleaf are the templates for the stencils. You can use these templates as they are, or enlarge them to suit your own furniture. Overleaf you'll find full instructions for applying the stencil in your chosen colour.

JAM POT COVERS

Brighten up plain jam jars by making super fringed covers for them. They are easy to make, and you can use fabric remnants left over from larger projects, such as the curtains, cushions or tablecloth.

MAKING A JAM POT COVER

Measure across the top of the jar and add 5cm (2in). Cut out a square of fabric this size. Make 3mm (⅛in) snips into the fabric all round the edges, and pull away the cross threads to fringe the fabric. Tie the fabric over the top of the jar with twine for a rustic finishing touch.

STENCIL MOTIF

STENCILLED TRAY

Coordinate kitchen accessories by stencilling them in the colours of the kitchen. Here, the wooden tray was painted blue, then stencilled in yellow to echo the yellow of the tablecloth.

STENCIL MOTIF

MATERIALS

Wooden tray

Sandpaper and primer

Tracing paper

Carbon paper

Stencilling card or acetate film

Emulsion paint for the base coat

Artists' acrylic paint for the stencil

Craft knife and cutting mat

Saucer

Masking tape

Pencil and ruler

Stencil brush

Clear varnish

1 PREPARING THE SURFACE
Sand the tray smooth and wipe it clean. Seal it with primer, if necessary, and leave it to dry. Paint the tray with two coats of emulsion paint.

2 TRANSFERRING THE DESIGN
Trace the design (left) on to tracing paper. Using the carbon paper, transfer the design centrally on to the card. If you are using acetate film, trace the design straight on to it.

3 CUTTING THE STENCIL
Tape the card or acetate to the cutting surface with masking tape. Using the craft knife, cut along the design lines. For long, curved lines, it is easier to move the stencil around as you work, rather than the blade.

4 POSITIONING THE STENCIL
Using the pencil and ruler, measure and mark the centre of one end of the tray so that you can centre the motif along it. Position the stencil and fix it in place with masking tape.

5 PAINTING THE STENCIL
Squeeze some acrylic paint into a saucer. Dilute it with water if necessary for a creamy consistency. Dip the stencil brush into the paint and dab off the excess on scrap paper. Apply the paint to the tray through the stencil.

Leave the paint to dry, then remove the stencil. Stencil the other end of the tray in the same way. For a protective finish, paint the tray with two or three coats of clear varnish.

Provençal Kitchen – Trimming shelves

Complete your cheerful yellow and blue Provençal kitchen with pretty frilled shelf edgings. For the finishing touches, decorate your table linen to match, and create decorative storage containers by wrapping wicker baskets with fabric remnants.

▼ Frilled shelf edgings add a pretty finishing touch to kitchen shelves. The deeper frill over the hob cleverly conceals the functional light fitting.

FRILLED SHELF EDGING

Use two of your mini-print kitchen fabrics to make these colourful shelf edgings. The narrow frill looks good on most shelves, or you can use the wide frill to conceal strip lights.

MATERIALS

Fabric for the trim

Second fabric for the frill

Matching sewing threads

Scissors

Tape measure

Self-adhesive touch-and-close spots (Velcro)

CUTTING LIST

From the trim fabric

● One 8cm (3¼in) wide strip the length of the shelf plus 2cm (¾in)

From the frill fabric

● *For a narrow frill*, one 9cm (3½in) wide strip 2½ times the length of the shelf

● *For a deep frill*, one 13cm (5in) wide strip 2½ times the length of the shelf

Note: join fabric strips together as necessary. Take 1cm (⅜in) seam allowances throughout.

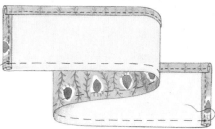

1 MAKING THE FRILL
Stitch a 1cm (⅜in) double hem along the short edges and lower long edge of the frill strip. Using a long machine stitch, sew a line of gathering stitches along the raw edge of the frill, 1cm (⅜in) from the edge.

► Coordinate plain white napkins with a bold yellow mini-print border and an embroidered motif, taken from the design used on the stencilled tray.

To recreate this look, cut the hems off ready-made napkins and transfer the motif (below) on to one corner. Work the design in satin stitch using a colour to tie in with your kitchen colour scheme. For the border, cut an 8cm (3in) wide fabric strip, long enough to go round the napkin plus 2cm (¾in), and attach it in the same way as binding, mitring it at the corners.

EMBROIDERY PATTERN

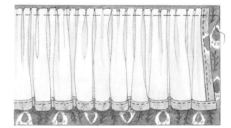

2 ADDING THE TRIM
Gather up the frill and pin it to the trim strip with the right sides together, leaving a 1cm (⅜in) overlap on the trim on each side of the frill. Stitch the seam.

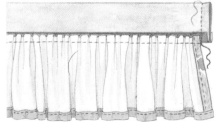

3 STITCHING THE SIDES
Press under the long unstitched edge of the trim by 1cm (⅜in). Fold the trim in half, with the right sides together, and stitch the sides, taking a 1cm (⅜in) seam allowance.

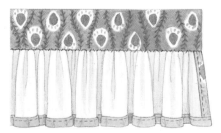

4 FINISHING THE TRIM
Turn the trim right side out and pin the folded edge to the frill seamline. Slipstitch it in place, enclosing the raw edges of the seam. Stick the frill to the front of the shelf with the self-adhesive touch-and-close spots.

FABRIC-WRAPPED BASKETS

Turn a plain wicker basket into a decorative storage container for the kitchen by wrapping it in fabric left over from larger sewing projects. You can cover the whole basket or just trim the handles and add a flirty bow.

COVERED BASKET

This basket has covered sides and a removable fabric-covered base. You'll need a basket, some large fabric scraps, thick card, scissors, a needle, thread and glue.

1 GETTING STARTED
Cut a piece of fabric large enough to wrap over the basket and reach down to the base inside. Lay out the fabric, wrong side up, and stand the basket in the centre.

2 WRAPPING THE BASKET
Fold the fabric over the basket sides, arranging it into even folds, and pin the folds on the outside of the basket to hold them. Arrange and pin the folds inside the basket in the same way. Trim away the excess fabric round the edges as necessary.

Use a needle and matching thread to secure the folds as close to the basket base as possible. If the basket has a loose weave, take the stitches through the basket as well. Remove the pins.

3 MAKING A BASE
Place the basket on the card and draw round it. Cut out the card, then trim it to fit the inside base of the basket. Using the card as a template, cut a piece of fabric 1.5cm (⅝in) larger all round.

Spread one side of the card with fabric adhesive and place this side centrally on to the wrong side of the fabric. Snip the fabric edge up to the card for ease, then turn this over the card and glue it down firmly. When the glue has dried, push the base down into the basket.

FABRIC-WRAPPED HANDLES

1 WRAPPING THE HANDLES
Cut a 12cm (4¾in) wide fabric strip, 120cm (48in) long. Fold it in half lengthways, with the right sides together and stitch the long edge. Turn the fabric right sides out and sew or stick one end to the base of the handle on one side. Wrap the strip tightly around the handle, overlapping each edge slightly. Trim off the excess fabric, tuck under the raw end and glue or stitch it in place.

▶ This fabric-woven basket is a useful accessory. To copy this idea, cut a long strip of fabric 10cm (4in) wide. Turn under a 1cm (⅜in) hem along each long edge and stitch it. Thread one end of the strip near the base of your basket from the inside to the outside, and thread it back to the inside under the upper rim of the basket. Continue round the basket, joining on new strips as necessary. Tie the ends together on the inside.

2 ADDING A BOW
Cut a 120 x 20cm (48 x 8in) fabric strip, and fold it in half lengthways with the right sides together. Stitch the ends on the diagonal, and stitch the long edge, leaving an opening at the centre. Trim the seam allowances at the corners. Turn the strip right sides out through the opening, then tuck in the raw edges at the opening and slipstitch the opening closed. Tie the strip in a bow around the handle.

Red Gingham Kitchen

For a vibrant kitchen, red and white checks are a classic combination, and are perfect to update a country-style kitchen. White walls and floor create a spacious look, while plain reds mixed with gingham and pine furniture add homely warmth.

In this room you can make:
- Gingham shelf trims
- Café curtains with a simple ruched heading
- A handy herb ring for fresh or dried herbs

Give new life to a plain pine dresser with some bright and cheerful checked fabric trims.

Make decorative kitchen accessories for your red and white kitchen, plus trim a wire basket.

Complete the kitchen with matching squashy buttoned squab cushions and a handy note board.

CREATING THE LOOK

The effect created in this kitchen is based on the cheerful contrast between the light, uncluttered areas of the plain white walls and floor, and the medley of bright reds and checks used for furnishings and accessories. Pine furniture has a sturdy, simple look which helps to balance these elements and provides an ideal background for the red and white fabrics.

With these strong basics you can have fun adding to the red and white theme with brightly coloured china, kitchenware and linen. You can also introduce accent colours, perhaps by adding splashes of deep green or yellow for table linen and china ware – plain colours like these provide a visual 'break' which complements the main colour theme.

One of the many advantages of this cheerful country style is its versatility. Modern accessories in chrome and glass will look just as good here as more traditional designs in natural wood, brass or terracotta. Rustic wire containers are another option for accessories; these come in quaint designs which suit this bright and cheerful version of the country style.

LINING DRESSER SHELVES

Gingham panels add a cheerful touch to dresser shelves, and provide a colourful backdrop for china displays and kitchen clutter. A checked trim, cut along the lower edge in a simple geometric pattern, provides a quick finishing touch to the shelf edges.

MATERIALS

Large check gingham fabric (see steps 1 and 5 for quantities, and allow extra fabric for any joins)

Stiff backing material such as buckram (see step 1 for quantity)

Medium or heavyweight iron-on interfacing (see step 5 for quantity)

Self-adhesive touch and close tabs or strips, such as Velcro

Fabric adhesive

Fabric marker pen

Sharp, pointed scissors

1 MEASURING UP FOR THE PANELS
Measure the width and depth of the dresser back between each shelf. Use these measurements to calculate how much backing material you'll need. To calculate how much main fabric you'll need, allow an extra 2.5cm (1in) all round each piece for the turnings.

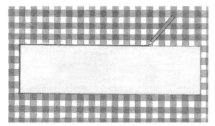

2 CUTTING OUT THE FABRIC
Draw the dimensions of each shelf back (excluding the turning allowances) on to the backing material. Cut out each panel just inside the drawn line to allow for the thickness of the fabric turnings. Note which panel goes behind each shelf.

Place the gingham on a flat surface with the wrong side facing upwards. Lay a backing panel over this, lining up the edges with the gingham checks, and draw round the outline. Cut out the fabric 2.5cm (1in) from the drawn edge. Repeat for the other panels.

3 COVERING THE PANELS
Lay the gingham flat, as before, and lay the backing panel in position over this. Spread adhesive round the edges of the panel. Start by folding the four corners on to the adhesive, dab a little more adhesive over these, then fold the turnings over and press them flat. Leave the glue to dry thoroughly.

DISPLAYING HERBS

For an attractive display, wind wide gingham ribbon round a bought vine garland and trim it with a bow, held in place with strong thread or florists' wire. In front of the bow, tie or sew on some garlic and chilli peppers. Slip fresh or dried sprigs of herbs into the garland, so that you can pull them out when you need them for cooking. Rosemary, thyme and sage were used here for their pungent aromas and attractive foliage. You can also add bay leaves and other strong-stemmed herbs.

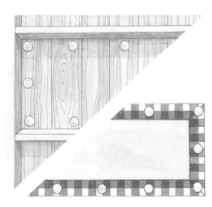

4 ATTACHING THE PANELS
Stick the touch and close tabs, (or small pieces cut from the strip), between the shelves at each corner of the dresser back, and at intervals along the width. Add the corresponding fastenings to the backs of the panels, then press each panel in place.

5 TRIMMING THE SHELF EDGES
Measure the width of each shelf. Cut strips of gingham two and a half checks deep by the width of each shelf. Iron interfacing to the wrong side of the strips. Along the top edge, press the line of half checks to the wrong side, then cut around the checks to shape the lower edge. Stick touch and close fastenings to the wrong sides, as shown, and press the trims into position along the shelf edges.

CAFE CURTAINS

Half curtains like these are ideal for blocking out an uninspiring view, and make a colourful alternative to nets when privacy is a priority. These cafe curtains have a novel addition – a matching pelmet. Made from unlined gingham, the curtain and frilled pelmet are simple to run up, as no curtain tapes or hooks are required.

The curtain and pelmet are made in the same way, and slotted on to poles through a casing. The fullness of the fabric creates an attractive frilled effect across the top hems.

MATERIALS

Gingham fabric (see step 2 for quantities)

Two 22mm (¾in) diameter wooden curtain poles and fittings

Matching sewing threads

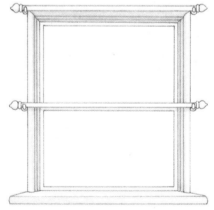

1 POSITIONING THE POLES
Fit the lower curtain pole halfway down the window, level with the top of any lower pane, and with the fittings outside the window frame. If the pole is too long, mark its required length with a pencil and use a small saw to cut it to length. Fit the pelmet pole across the top of the window frame.

2 ESTIMATING FABRIC AMOUNTS
Measure the window. For *the curtain,* cut and join fabric widths to make a piece twice the width of the window by half the length of the window plus 28cm (11in) for the top frill and the hem. Neaten the seam allowances with zigzag or straight stitch.

For *the pelmet*, cut and join fabric widths to make a piece twice the width of the window by about one third of the depth of the main curtain plus 28cm (11in). Neaten the seam allowances as before.

3 STITCHING THE SIDE HEMS
Make side hems on the curtain by folding the raw edges to the wrong side twice by 1cm (⅜in). Stitch the hems by hand or machine.

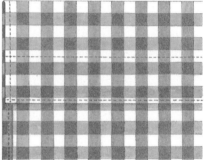

4 MAKING THE TOP FRILL
Along the top of the curtain, turn 20cm (8in) to the wrong side, in line with a row of checks, then turn the raw edge under by 1cm (⅜in) and press it with an iron.

Pin and stitch across the curtain along the lower folded edge. Stitch another line 4cm (1½in) above this to make a casing. (Increase or reduce this measurement if you are using a thicker or thinner curtain pole.)

5 HANGING THE CURTAIN
Thread the pole through the casing, and hang it in position. Pin the lower hem to mark its position, then remove the curtain from the pole. Turn under the lower raw edge, and stitch it by hand or machine.

6 MAKING THE PELMET
Repeat steps 3-5 to make the pelmet, then hang the pelmet and curtain at the window.

Red Gingham Kitchen – Accessories

Liven up your kitchen with jolly red and white checked
accessories, like a fringed tablecloth and matching napkins.
Complete the look with inexpensive modern touches, such as
a wire basket and a set of homemade metal napkin rings.

▼Red gingham, teamed
with cheerful red and
white, is an attractive
combination for eye-
catching accessories in a
rustic style kitchen.

FRINGED TABLECLOTH

Nothing could be simpler than this pretty fringed tablecloth. It's made from a single width of large-check gingham, with decorative patches of smaller checks.

The finished tablecloth is 140cm (54in) square. If you want a larger tablecloth, join as many fabric lengths as you need *before* fringing the edges.

To complete the effect, make matching napkins from 45cm (18in) squares of the smaller check fabric, and fringe them round the edges to coordinate with the tablecloth.

MATERIALS

1.4m (1½yd) of 140cm (54in) wide large-check gingham fabric

70cm (¾yd) of 140cm (54in) wide small-check gingham fabric

Matching sewing thread

Strong needle or pin

▼ **The fringed tablecloth links the bold check on the dresser and the smaller check of the other accessories.**

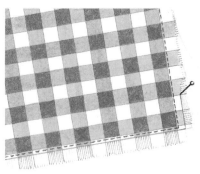

1 CUTTING OUT THE CLOTH
Trim away the fabric selvedges level with the edge of a line of checks. To cut an accurate square, fold the fabric diagonally and line up one side edge with a row of checks on one end. Trim the fabric along the edges of the checks.

2 SECURING THE EDGES
Machine stitch 2.5cm (1in) in from the cut edge (or to the depth of one large check) all round the tablecloth. Secure the thread ends with backstitch. Snip to the stitches at 5cm (2in) intervals to make it easier to fringe.

3 FRINGING THE EDGES
Using a strong pin or needle, gently pull away the cross threads on each edge of the cloth to within 3mm (⅛in) of the stitched line. Gently tease the fringed edges straight with the point of the pin or needle.

4 FRINGING THE PATCHES
Cut five 32cm (12½in) squares (to the nearest check) from small-check gingham, and fringe the edges (see steps 2-3).

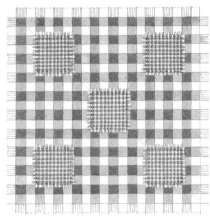

5 ADDING THE PATCHES
Fold the tablecloth into quarters and mark the centre. Lay the tablecloth out flat again and pin one fringed patch centrally over the centre mark. Measure diagonally across the cloth and pin the other four squares at equal distances along these lines. Topstitch the squares in place on the tablecloth, then remove the pins.

MAKING THE NAPKINS

Make matching napkins from 45cm (18in) squares of small-check gingham, following the same method as used for the FRINGED TABLECLOTH, steps 1-3. You can make six napkins from 90cm (1yd) of 140cm (54in) wide fabric.

COILED WIRE NAPKIN RINGS

Imitate the style of modern kitchen designs with these fashionable bead-trimmed napkin rings – they're made from wire coat hangers.

MATERIALS

For each ring:

A wire coat hanger

Small bolt cutters

A pole or strong tube with a 3.5cm (1⅜in) diameter to shape the wire

Thick gloves such as oven or gardening gloves

Two wooden beads

Instant bonding glue

1 CUTTING THE WIRE
Using bolt cutters, snip the lower, straight length from the wire coat hanger. You'll use this to make the napkin ring.

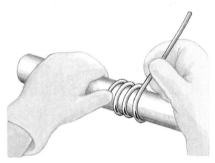

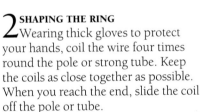

2 SHAPING THE RING
Wearing thick gloves to protect your hands, coil the wire four times round the pole or strong tube. Keep the coils as close together as possible. When you reach the end, slide the coil off the pole or tube.

3 ADDING THE BEADS
Cut the ends of the coil level with each other, leaving two complete coils in between. Spread a little glue on to each end of the coil and push a coloured wooden bead on to it. Leave the glue to dry thoroughly.

OVEN GLOVE

A practical oven glove with a deep cuff in a coordinated fabric makes a colourful accessory in a kitchen. The fabric quantities given here are sufficient to make a pair of gloves.

MATERIALS

40cm (½yd) of 90cm (36in) wide plain or patterned red cotton fabric

40cm (½yd) of 90cm (36in) wide gingham fabric

50cm (⅝yd) medium or heavyweight polyester wadding

Matching sewing threads

Paper to make a pattern

1 square = 5cm (2in)

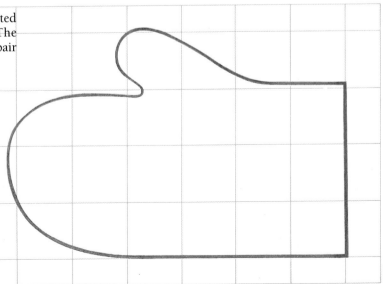

MAKING THE OVEN GLOVES

1 CUTTING THE PATTERN
Scale up the pattern and transfer it to paper. To make one glove, cut the pattern twice from red fabric, wadding and gingham, adding 1cm (⅜in) all round for seam allowances.

3 MAKING THE LINING
Stitch the gingham linings together in the same way as the main pieces (see step 2). Fit the gingham lining inside the glove.

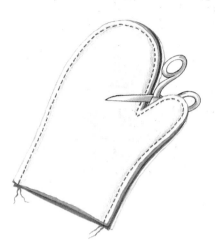

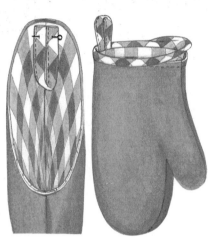

2 ASSEMBLING THE PIECES
Place the red fabric pieces right sides together, then pin a wadding piece on to each side. Stitch round the curved edges through all four layers, taking 1cm (⅜in) seams. Snip into the angle at the base of the thumb, so that the glove will sit flat when turned out. Turn the glove right sides out.

4 BINDING THE EDGE
Cut a 19cm (7½in) bias strip of fabric to make a loop to hang up the glove. Fold in the raw edges and topstitch the binding close to the edge. Fold the strip in half and pin it to the side seam. Stitch the binding to the inside of the glove, then turn it up and topstitch it in place on the right side.

CHILD'S APRON

Scale up the pattern (below right) to make a bright and cheerful child's wipe-clean apron.

MATERIALS
60cm (⅝yd) of 140cm (54in) wide PVC fabric

1.8m (2yd) of 2.5cm (1in) wide matching woven tape

23cm (¼yd) broderie anglaise trim

Two 'D' rings, or two curtain rings

Matching sewing threads

A dressmakers' marker pen

Sticky tape

Talcum powder

1 CUTTING OUT THE APRON
Scale up the pattern and transfer it to paper. Lay the pattern on to the back of the PVC and hold it in place with pieces of sticky tape. (Pins would mark the surface.) Draw round the pattern with the marker pen and cut it out. Make small 6mm (¼in) snips at 2.5cm (1in) intervals along the curved apron sides for ease. Cut a rectangle, as marked, for the pocket.

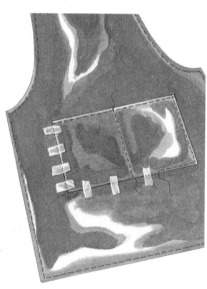

2 SEWING THE APRON
Turn under 1cm (⅜in) hems along the apron edges and stitch them in place. Turn under and stitch the top edge of the pocket. Fold under the edges on the other three sides of the pocket. Tape the pocket to the apron and topstitch it in place, removing the sticky tape as you stitch. Sew down the centre of the pocket to divide it into two smaller pockets.

3 ADDING THE TIES

Cut a 9cm (3½in) length of tape and slip on the two 'D' rings or curtain rings. Fold the tape into a loop and stitch it on to one side of the apron top. Stitch a 76cm (30in) length of tape on to the other side of the apron and thread it through the 'D' rings. Cut the remaining tape in half, and stitch a piece on to each side of the apron.

4 ADDING THE TRIM

Press under the raw ends of the broderie anglaise trim to neaten it. Machine stitch the trim across the top of the apron.

1 square = 5cm (2in)

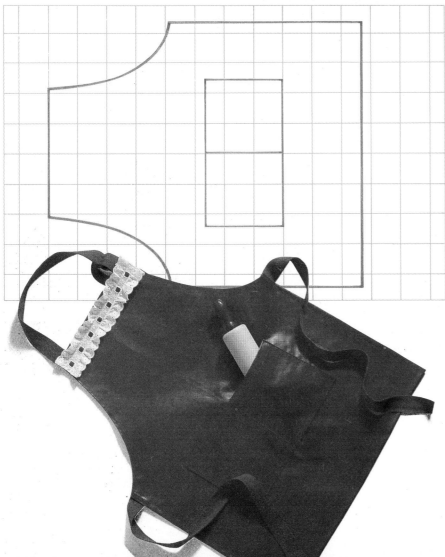

RIBBON TRIMMED TOWELS

Coloured ribbon makes an attractive coordinating trim for plain towels. Use it to trim new towels or give a new lease of life to an old towel.

Trimming the towels

Cut away the selvedges and woven edges of the towel. Fold a length of ribbon in half lengthways and press it. Tack the ribbon over the raw edges of the towel, neatening the corners by folding the ribbon into mitred angles Machine stitch the ribbon in place with a matching thread.

SEWING PVC *Tip*

Dust the sewing machine footplate lightly with talcum powder before stitching the apron. This prevents the PVC sticking to the footplate.

FINISHING TOUCHES

WOVEN BASKET

Make an instant trim for a wire or wicker basket with rag strips. Simply rip strips of fabric across the width of a fabric length, and fray the edges slightly as described for the FRINGED TABLECLOTH, step 3. Weave these strips of fabric round the edges of the basket. Use strips of the same width for a neat effect, or mix strips of different widths for a casual effect, as on the basket, shown left.

QUICK JAM POT COVERS

Use pinking shears to cut 20cm (8in) diameter circles from gingham to make pretty cover-ups for lids on jam pots and jars of relishes, like the ones below. Tie the lid covers on with matching ribbon.

MILK JUG COVER

Make a traditional milk jug cover from a gingham circle, neatened with machine zigzag. Work two rows of double crochet round the edge, then weight the cover with wooden or glass beads.

Red Gingham Kitchen – Padded cushion

You can make all kinds of colour-matched accessories for your red gingham kitchen. Dress up a plain kitchen chair with a comfortable seat pad, and brighten shelves and work tops with cheerful gingham containers and fragrant sachets.

▼A cheerful red and white gingham cushion makes a pine kitchen chair more comfortable. The cushion is buttoned and tied in place with generous bows.

BUTTONED SEAT PAD

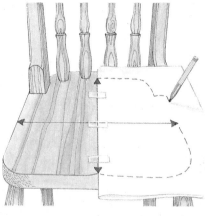

A buttoned seat pad gives comfort and style to a traditional pine chair. This one is tied to the chair back with gingham ties, but you could use lengths of ribbon or cotton tape instead.

Stitch 1cm (⅜in) seams throughout – there's no need to allow extra fabric for seam allowances as the pad needs to be slightly smaller than the chair.

MATERIALS

For each pad to fit an average size chair seat:

1m (1⅛yd) of 140cm (54in) wide large check gingham

46cm (½yd) heavyweight polyester wadding

Ten 2cm (¾in) diameter easy cover buttons

Scraps of plain red fabric or gingham to cover the buttons

Matching sewing threads

Dressmakers' marker pen

Tape measure

Pencil, newspaper and sticky tape to make a pattern

1 MAKING A PATTERN
Measure across the width and depth of the chair seat to find the centre point. Mark this point lightly on the chair with a pencil.

Fold a sheet of newspaper in half, and tape the fold along the centre of the chair. Mark the edge of the chair on the paper, then remove the paper and cut out the shape through both layers. Place the pattern on the chair seat, and adjust the fit if necessary.

2 CUTTING THE FABRIC
Use the pattern to cut two seat sections from gingham, matching checks where possible. Then cut two seat sections from wadding.

For the ties, cut four 20cm (8in) strips across the width of the remaining fabric.

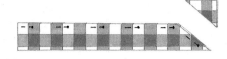

3 MAKING THE TIES
Fold each tie piece in half lengthways, with right sides facing, and pin it together. Cut it at an angle at one end. Stitch the angled and long edges, and turn the tie right side out. Press it flat.

4 ATTACHING THE WADDING
Place each gingham seat section right side up over a wadding section and tack them together. Pin the straight ends of two tie strips to each side of one gingham section, matching the raw edges.

5 ASSEMBLING THE SEAT PAD
Pin the other seat section on top, with the right sides of the gingham facing. Stitch together, leaving a gap for turning out. Turn out, and slipstitch the gap closed.

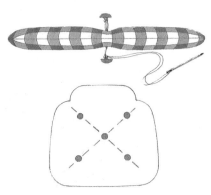

6 ADDING THE BUTTONS
Cover the buttons. Measure and mark the centre of the cushion. Using a double thread, stitch a button to the centre and take the thread to the other side. Thread on another button and stitch back through to the first button, as shown. Continue stitching until the buttons are secure.

Stitch on the other buttons in the same way.

Colour Theme Bathroom

Blue and white are favourite colours for a bathroom. Add warmth to your bathroom with natural pine and brass accessories. Make a handy sponge bag and matching cotton-wool holder to help you keep things tidy.

▼ Blue and white will give a light, airy feel to even the smallest bathroom. Add pretty accessories in warm colours for a welcoming touch.

◄ Turn your bath salts into eyecatching features by layering them in clear glass containers.

► Cover plain storage boxes with wallpaper to coordinate them with your bathroom colour scheme.

CREATING THE LOOK

Blue and white is a lovely colour combination for a fresh bathroom scheme. Large areas of white give the bathroom an open, clean look and help to reflect light, while blue creates a relaxing mood which is ideal if you like to take long, lingering baths.

Plain white tiles cover most of the walls in this bathroom. These are inexpensive and widely available, and mean that you can change the colour scheme later, if you wish, without retiling. If you like, you can add decorative detailing with a border of

patterned tiles round the top or at dado rail height.

Blue and white are cool colours, so add warm accents, like the pine mirror and shelf, and choose brass or gold coloured fittings rather than stainless steel or silver which can look cold.

SPONGE BAG

Make this practical, quilted sponge bag in pretty blue and white floral fabric with a coordinating lining. It's 30 x 15cm (12 x 6in), so it's large enough for all your accessories.

MATERIALS

50cm (½yd) of 90cm (36in) wide main fabric

50cm (½yd) of 90cm (36in) wide lining fabric

50cm (½yd) of 90cm (36in) wide mediumweight wadding

30cm (12in) zip

2m (2¼yd) of 2.5cm (1in) wide bias binding

Threads to match the fabric and binding

CUTTING LIST

From main fabric
- One 45 x 30cm (17¾ x 12in) rectangle for the main panel
- Two 15 x 10cm (6 x 4in) rectangles for the end panels

From the lining fabric
- Three rectangles the same size as the main fabric rectangles

From the wadding
- Three rectangles the same size as the main fabric rectangles

Note: take 1.5cm (⅝in) seam allowances unless otherwise stated.

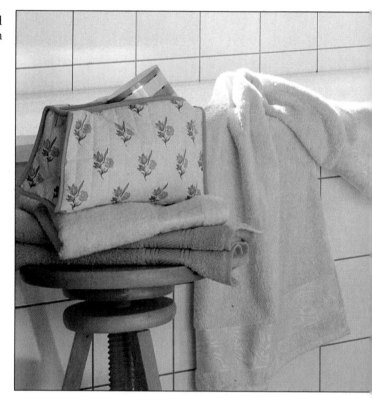

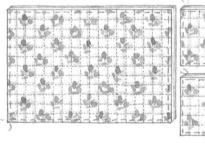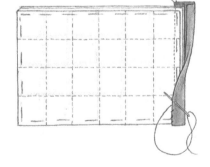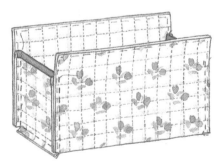

1 QUILTING THE FABRIC
Sandwich the large wadding panel between the large lining panel and the large fabric panel, with the right sides out. Tack or machine stitch close to the outer edges. Machine quilt straight vertical and horizontal rows, spaced 2.5cm (1in) apart. Repeat to quilt the two smaller panels.

2 BINDING THE END PANELS
Cut a 10cm (4in) length of bias binding. Unfold one edge of the binding and pin it to the top, short edge of one small panel, with the raw edges level and the right sides together. Stitch along the binding foldline. Fold the long free edge of the binding to the wrong side of the panel and oversew the fold to the previous stitching line. Repeat to bind the other small panel.

3 SHAPING THE BAG
With the wrong sides together, pin the centre of the lower edge of one small panel to the centre of one long edge of the large panel. Take the fabric up round the sides of the small panel and pin it in place, snipping into the corners. Tack the seam close to the edge. Tack the other small panel to the opposite edge of the large panel in the same way.

Peach, pink, apricot or yellow towels will also add a warming touch, and you can add other small items in the same colours, like pretty guest soaps, and bath salts in clear glass containers.

4 BINDING THE SIDES
Bind the tacked seams as in step 2, continuing the binding up to the top of the main panel. At the corners, pivot the stitching and tuck any excess binding into tiny pleats.

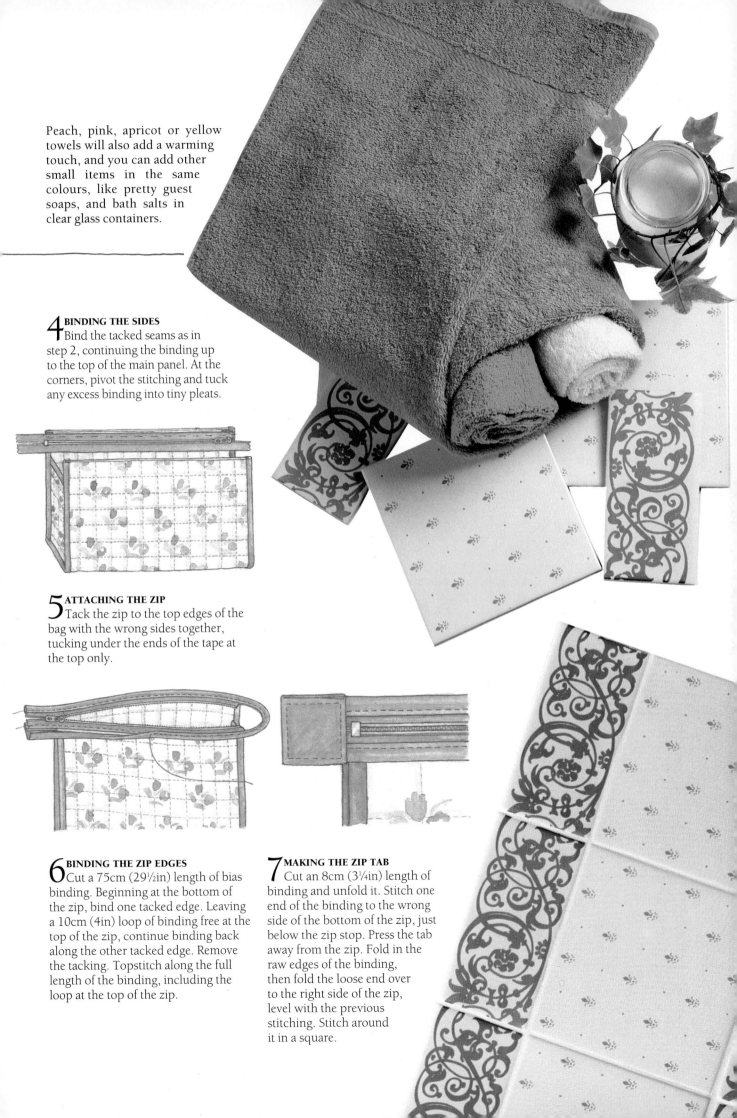

5 ATTACHING THE ZIP
Tack the zip to the top edges of the bag with the wrong sides together, tucking under the ends of the tape at the top only.

6 BINDING THE ZIP EDGES
Cut a 75cm (29½in) length of bias binding. Beginning at the bottom of the zip, bind one tacked edge. Leaving a 10cm (4in) loop of binding free at the top of the zip, continue binding back along the other tacked edge. Remove the tacking. Topstitch along the full length of the binding, including the loop at the top of the zip.

7 MAKING THE ZIP TAB
Cut an 8cm (3¼in) length of binding and unfold it. Stitch one end of the binding to the wrong side of the bottom of the zip, just below the zip stop. Press the tab away from the zip. Fold in the raw edges of the binding, then fold the loose end over to the right side of the zip, level with the previous stitching. Stitch around it in a square.

COTTON-WOOL HOLDER

Make a cotton-wool holder to go with your sponge bag.
It's 12cm (4¾in) high and 16cm (6¼in) in diameter.

MATERIALS

20cm (¼yd) of 90cm (36in) wide main fabric

20cm (¼yd) of 90cm (36in) wide lining fabric

20cm (¼yd) of 90cm (36in) wide mediumweight wadding

2m (2¼yd) of 2.5cm (¾in) wide bias binding

Matching thread

CUTTING LIST

From main fabric
● One 50 x 12cm (19¾ x 4¾in) rectangle for the side panel
● Two 16cm (6¼in) diameter circles for the base and lid

From lining fabric
● Two circles and one rectangle the same size as the main fabric pieces

From wadding
● Two circles and one rectangle the same size as the main fabric pieces
Note: take seam allowances of 1cm (⅜in) unless otherwise stated.

1 PREPARING THE PIECES
Cut one of the main fabric circles in half to make two semi-circles. Repeat with one wadding and one lining circle. Sandwich each wadding piece between the corresponding lining and main fabric pieces with the right sides out, and quilt them as for the SPONGE BAG, step 1. Repeat to quilt the rectangular panel in the same way.

2 ATTACHING THE SIDES
Fold the quilted rectangle in half widthways with the right sides facing and stitch the short edges together, taking a 1cm (⅜in) seam allowance. Press the seam open.

Pin the quilted rectangle to the circle with the wrong sides facing, and tack them together close to the edges. Bind the edges as for the SPONGE BAG, step 2.

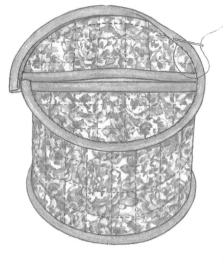

3 ATTACHING THE LID
Bind the straight edge of each semi-circle as for the SPONGE BAG, step 2. With the wrong sides together, pin the semi-circles to the top of the cotton-wool holder, with their straight, bound edges matching. Tack round the edge, then cover the seam with binding.

◄ **Bath salts come in a range of pretty colours, so why not put them on display? Pour layers of bath salts in different colours into a jar or bowl to store in the bathroom. If you like, use a long spoon to drag the layers into each other, as shown in the largest jar.**

Colour Theme Bathroom – Decorated towels

Complete your fresh blue and white bathroom with pretty
appliquéd towels, some handy fabric-covered storage boxes and a
smart Roman blind. The blind has a bold striped border, mitred at
the corners for a neat finish.

▼ These super towels have
stylish cutwork designs
made with lace motifs.
You can quite easily
appliqué a towel in this
way in less than an hour.

APPLIQUED TOWELS

Add a touch of luxury to plain towels, or make a guest towel extra special, with crisp lace motifs. And your towels will cost a fraction of the price of shop-bought ones. Choose large motifs with cut-away sections, or arrange several motifs together on the towel with gaps in between which you can cut away.

MATERIALS
Towel

Lace motifs

Matching threads

Small, sharp, pointed scissors

Pins

1 STITCHING THE MOTIFS
Pin the motifs on to the towel. Using close machine zigzag, stitch round the edge of each motif and round any sections to be cut away.

2 CUTTING AWAY THE BACKING
Turn the towel over and carefully insert the point of the scissors into the towelling in the areas you wish to cut away. Snip away the towelling between the lines of zigzag stitching.

▶ Use household paint suitable for woodwork, and ready-made stencils which feature small, detailed motifs, to decorate natural wooden hair and nail brushes and other small accessories.

ROMAN BLIND

If your bathroom has a window make this smart Roman blind from coordinating patterned fabric, with a striped fabric for the 7.5cm (3in) wide border. For the lining, choose a plain, pale-coloured fabric, such as white or cream, to let in maximum light.

Before you make the blind, decide if you want it to hang inside or outside the window recess, then measure up accordingly.

MATERIALS

Main fabric

Striped border fabric

Lining fabric (optional)

Iron-on interfacing (optional)

Matching thread

Austrian blind tape and cord

Touch-and-close tape the width of the blind

2.5 x 2.5cm (1 x 1in) wooden batten the width of the blind

Screw eyes

Screws and wall plugs to attach the batten to the wall

Cleat

CUTTING LIST

From main fabric
- One rectangle the finished width of the blind by the length plus 2cm (¾in)

From lining fabric (optional)
- One rectangle the same size as the main fabric rectangle

From striped border fabric
- One 17cm (6¾in) wide strip twice the length of the blind plus its width plus 5cm (2in) – join pieces as necessary, using the largest piece in the centre

From iron-on interfacing
- One 17cm (6¾in) wide strip the same length as the border strip; butt pieces together as necessary

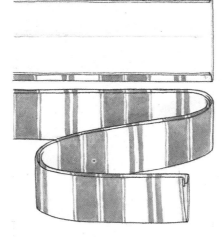

1 PREPARING THE BORDER
Iron the interfacing on to the wrong side of the border strip to prevent the main fabric showing through. Press the strip in half lengthways, with the wrong sides together, and press under 1cm (⅜in) along each long edge.

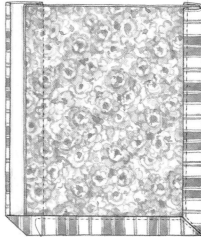

2 ATTACHING THE BORDER
Tack the lining and main fabric together with wrong sides facing. Tack the border strip to the side and lower edges of the fabrics in the same way as binding, mitring the corners. Topstitch it in place. Topstitch or slipstitch the mitred corners to hold them in place. Trim the ends of the border level with the top of the main fabric, if necessary.

3 FINISHING THE TOP
Working on the wrong side of the blind, turn down 2cm (¾in) at the top and pin it. Stitch the soft part of the touch-and-close tape over the turning, covering the raw fabric edge.

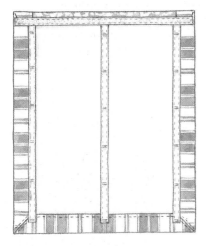

4 ATTACHING THE TAPES
Stitch a length of blind tape to each side edge of the blind on the wrong side, level with the inner edge of the border. Make sure each row of tape starts with a loop at the bottom of the blind. Stitch additional lengths of tape down the blind, evenly spaced at roughly 40cm (16in) intervals.

5 PREPARING THE WINDOW
Fix a cleat to the wall on one side of the window. Fix the batten above the window and stick the rough side of the touch-and-close tape to the front. Fit a screw eye to the underside of the batten to correspond with the top of each strip of tape on the blind.

6 HANGING THE BLIND
Starting at the opposite end of the blind to the cleat, knot the cord to the lowest loop on the tape and thread it up through every other loop on the tape. Leave enough cord to pass across the top of the blind and down to the cleat. Repeat with the remaining tapes.

Hang the blind on the batten by pressing the touch-and-close tape together. Thread the cord through the screw eyes to the cleat. Pull the cords to raise the blind, then tie the cords to the cleat to secure it.

▲ Paper-covered boxes make great storage containers for bathroom clutter. You can cover any cardboard boxes, such as shoe boxes or hat boxes, or even boxes you've made yourself. Use thick paper, like the wallpaper used here, to cover the box – it will provide extra strength and cover any writing on the box.

Marine Theme Bathroom

Give your bathroom a marine theme by decorating it in soft shades of aqua and silver. Stencil shell motifs on the walls and curtains to develop the theme, and add a touch of fantasy by decorating the furniture with shell 'mouldings'.

In this room you can make:
- Shell-stencilled motifs
- A shell cushion
- Embroidered towels
- Furniture decorated with real shells

Stencil shell motifs on the walls, and line a laundry basket.

Decorate a chair and mirror with shells and make a shell cushion.

Make a bath mat, embroider towels and dress a window.

AQUA SCHEME

This bathroom is so cool and inviting that you'll feel rested the moment you step into it. It's based on a one-colour scheme and is embellished with stencilled and embroidered shell motifs to emphasize the seaside theme.

The colour scheme works by using three shades of the main colour, starting with the deep aqua carpet, through the mid aqua panelling to the pale walls above. It's a one-colour scheme which works well with an ordinary white bathroom suite, like the one shown here. If you have a coloured bathroom suite, you can adapt the look accordingly – use shades of green with an avocado suite, or warm pinks with a pink suite.

An inexpensive clear plastic shower curtain, stencilled with silver shells, helps to lighten the effect, and provides a link with the chrome fittings. Silver embroidery on the towels also repeats the sheen of the chrome.

If you don't want to redecorate your whole bathroom, you can use just some of the ideas here to give your existing scheme a face-lift. The stencilled shower curtain, for example, would suit any bathroom, while the novelty bath mat – in the shape of a shell – would appeal to children.

▼ Use these four motifs as templates for the stencils. They are all full size – as used in the bathroom.

DECORATING THE WALLS

Start your aqua bathroom by painting the walls and ceiling in light aqua silk emulsion. Paint the window frame and door in light aqua satinwood, and use mid aqua satinwood for the dado panelling and door frame. To finish, add a dark aqua carpet (or paint bare floorboards in dark aqua).

SCALLOP BORDER

Create a border for your bathroom by stencilling the scallop design above your tongue and groove panelling.

MATERIALS

Mid aqua emulsion paint

Stencil card

Soft synthetic bath sponge

Craft knife

Saucer

Tracing paper

Old newspaper

STENCILLING THE BORDER

Prepare the stencil and plan the position of the motifs. Try out a few variations before you make a final decision. Fix the stencil in place with masking tape, and pour a small amount of paint into the saucer. Using the sponge, apply paint lightly through the stencil. Repeat to stencil all the motifs, wiping the back of the stencil each time.

QUICK BORDER *Tip*

If you're placing the motifs above a dado, try this quick method: cut out two 25cm (10in) squares of stencil card. Centre the motifs on the card, then cut them out.

Position one stencil so the base edge rests on the dado, and tape it in place. Tape the second stencil next to it. Stencil one motif, remove the stencil then tape it beside the adjoining one, so that you are always ready to stencil the next motif.

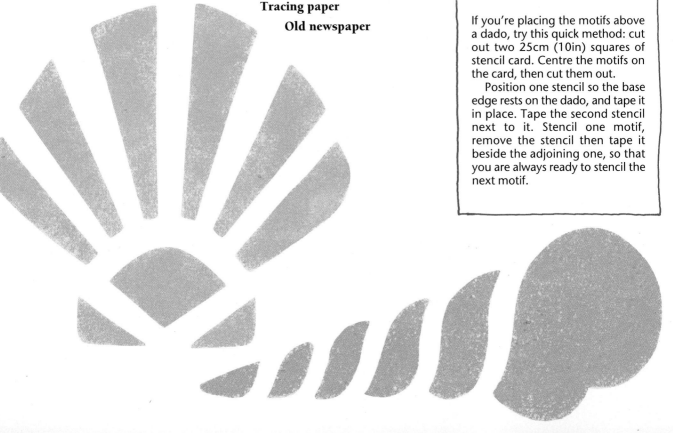

STENCILLED SHOWER CURTAIN

Use metallic spray paint to decorate a clear plastic shower curtain with silver shells. Spray paint is very quick to use, but it can be messy, so make sure you protect surrounding surfaces with plenty of newspaper or plastic sheeting and wear old clothing. If the weather is good, work outdoors.

MATERIALS

Clear plastic shower curtain

Stencil card

Tracing paper

Two cans of silver car spray paint

Rubber gloves

Cellulose thinner to remove painting mistakes

Paper tissues

Low-tack spray adhesive

Solvent

Masking tape

Newspaper or protective sheeting

Protective clothing and face mask (optional)

1 PREPARING TO STENCIL
Trace the stencils on to card at least 38cm (15in) square. Stretch the curtain on a flat surface in a well-ventilated area and protect surrounding areas.

2 PLANNING THE DESIGN
Decide which side of the curtain the border should run down. Measure from the shower rail down to the top of the bath – the border sits just above it. Mark the position on the curtain with tape.

3 STARTING THE BORDER
Spray the back of the border stencil with low-tack adhesive, and put it at the top of the curtain. Following the manufacturer's instructions, spray the stencil. Remove the stencil. Clean off any excess paint with thinner and a tissue; remove any excess adhesive with solvent.

4 COMPLETING THE STENCILLING
Reposition the stencil further down the curtain, leaving space for a different motif in between if desired; stencil it. Repeat until you've completed the border. Use the picture as a guide to stencils on the rest of the curtain, varying their angles for greater variety.

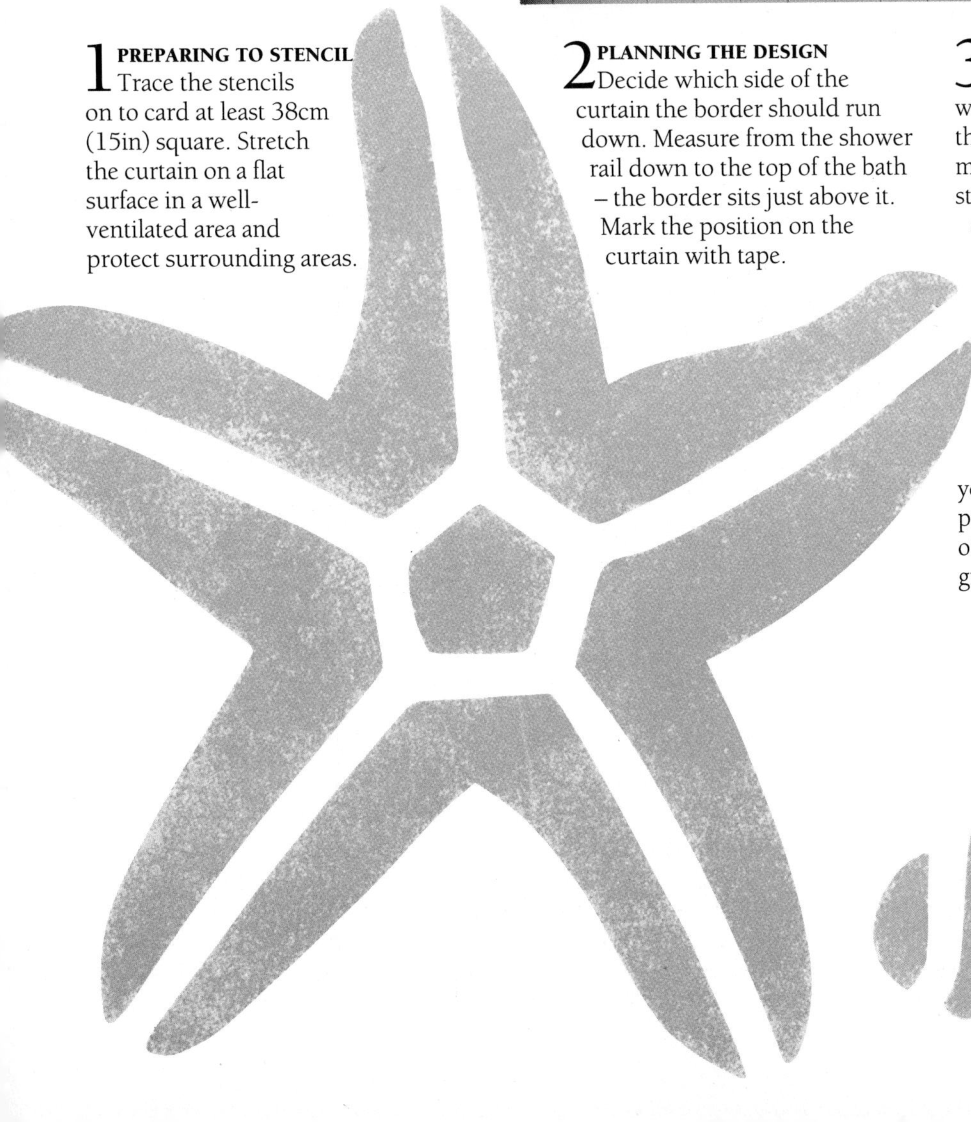

LAUNDRY BASKET

This attractive laundry basket is colour graded with aqua paint and lined with a toning cotton draw-string bag.

PAINTING THE BASKET

Paint the base and two thirds of the way up the sides with a mid aqua emulsion. Then use light aqua emulsion to paint the rest. When the paint is dry, lightly spray the basket all over with silver paint to give it a pearly sheen.

MAKING THE LINING

MATERIALS

Cotton fabric (see CUTTING LIST for quantities)

Matching sewing threads

Paper to make a pattern

Tailors' chalk

Silver car spray paint

Two large shells (optional)

CUTTING LIST

For lining
- Cut a rectangle of fabric to measurement (A) plus 3cm (1¼in) by (B) plus 22cm (8¾in) – see the diagram below left.
- Cut a circle of fabric the size of the base – seam allowances aren't needed.

For ties and draw-string
- Cut a 3 x 40cm (1¼ x 15in) strip for each tie.
- Cut a 7cm (2¾in) wide strip the circumference of basket plus 50cm (20in).

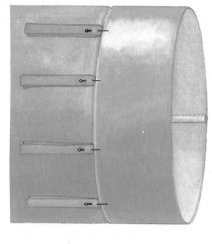

1 MAKING THE LINING
For a neat, strong finish, use French seams. Machine stitch the lining sides to form a tube.

To stitch the base with a French seam, gather one end of the tube to fit the base and, with wrong sides facing, stitch them together. Turn the lining to the wrong side and stitch the base seam again, enclosing the raw edges.

2 MAKING THE TIES
With right sides facing, stitch together the long edges of each strip, taking 1cm (⅜in) seams. Turn the ties to the right sides. Tuck in the raw edges at the ends and slipstitch them in place. Press the ties.
Note: eight ties were used here.

3 ADDING THE TIES
The ties are stitched into a pleat in the lining. To position the pleat, put the lining in the basket and, using tailors' chalk, mark the edge of the basket on the lining.

Right sides together, fold the lining back along the the chalk line and press it. Press the ties in half and position them so the folded edge aligns with the fold in the lining. Stitch 1cm (⅜in) from the fold, catching in the ties.

4 PREPARING THE TOP EDGE
Wrong sides together, fold back the top edge to make an 11cm (4¼in) hem. Turn in the raw edge and press the hem. This will help you to position the slot.

5 MAKING A SLOT AND CASING
Cut a 5cm (2in) square from scrap fabric. Position it on the right side, so that the lower edge sits 1cm (⅜in) below the hem edge. Fold the hem out of the way and stitch a 3cm (1¼in) slot through the patch and the top fabric only. Clip to the corners. Turn the patch to the wrong side and press it. Topstitch around the slot on the right side.

Machine stitch the hem, close to the folded edge. Stitch a second row 5cm (2in) above the first.

6 ADDING THE DRAWSTRING
Make the drawstring in the same way as the ties (step 2), and thread it through the casing. Put the lining in the basket and hold it in place by pushing the ties through the basket weave and tieing them in bows.

Spray paint the shells in silver, drill a hole through each one and then tie them to the ends of the draw-string. To stop the drill slipping, put a piece of masking tape on the shell.

Marine Theme Bathroom – Bathroom furniture

Real shell decorations complement the marine theme of this fresh aqua bathroom. Paint the shells and pearlize them with silver spray – they'll transform your furniture and bathroom accessories into fantasy pieces.

▼ **Paint a bathroom chair in aqua, then give it a pearly sheen with a light spray of silver paint. Continue the theme with a shell-shaped aqua cushion.**

SHELL MIRROR

Turn a simple framed mirror into a magical looking-glass with a cluster of seashells and some aqua and silver paint. Most of the shells are painted so these can be quite ordinary, but try to find a few large, well-formed shells for the centre of the shell arrangement.

Use aqua emulsion and paint the frame and the shells separately – the paint can dissolve the glue if you stick the shells on first. Once the shells are in place, spray the frame lightly with silver paint, then add a few unpainted pearly shells for a natural look.

Buy seashells and starfish from specialist shell suppliers, or collect your own from the beach – even damaged shells will be useful.

MATERIALS

Mirror with a sturdy wooden frame

Starfish and various seashells, including small pearly shells

Epoxy resin adhesive or a hot glue gun

Mid aqua emulsion

Silver car spray paint

Thinners

Small household paintbrushes

Fine grade sandpaper

Masking tape

Newspaper

1 PREPARING THE FRAME
Make sure the frame is firm, and that any paint is smooth and stable. If necessary, remove old paint with paint stripper. Sand the frame to remove any remaining paint and to provide a key for the new paint, then wipe it with a cloth to remove dust.

2 PAINTING THE FRAME
Cover the work surface with newspaper. Mask off the mirror by cutting the newspaper slightly smaller than the glass and sticking it on with masking tape. Position the tape level with, but not overlapping the inside edge of the frame.

Apply a coat of aqua paint and leave it to dry. Sand the frame gently, then apply a second coat of paint and leave this to dry.

3 PAINTING THE SHELLS
Use your smallest brush to paint the shells one at a time, but leave the small pearly shells unpainted. Work the paint sparingly but thoroughly into the surface contours. Leave the shells to dry on scrap paper. Repeat if necessary, and leave the paint to dry completely.

4 ARRANGING THE SHELLS

Lay the mirror on a flat surface and arrange the shells attractively on the frame. Place some shells side by side, and overlap others, using the best shells as focal points. When you are pleased with the effect, put the shells to one side in the same arrangement.

5 ADDING THE SHELLS

Remove the painted shells from the arrangement one at a time, starting with the central shells, and glue them on to the mirror, applying adhesive to the parts of the shells which will touch the frame. Continue building up the design in this way. Do not add the pearly shells yet – they will be added after the frame has been painted silver.

6 SPRAYING WITH SILVER PAINT

Protect the surrounding areas with newspaper. Prop up the mirror vertically and spray it lightly with the silver paint using an even, sweeping motion. Leave it to dry, then apply a second coat, changing the direction of the spray slightly to create shaded effects. When the paint is dry, remove the paper and tape.

7 ADDING PEARLY SHELLS

Arrange a few small pearly shells in between and on top of the painted shells, then group clusters of two or three tiny pearly shells together in the same way. Glue them in place.

▶ Turn a large, flat shell into a glamorous soap dish by painting it with aqua emulsion to match your bathroom. Then, lightly spray it with silver paint for a pearlized effect, and stick a cluster of small pearly shells at the base for a pretty finish.

BATHROOM CHAIR

Take a pretty wooden chair and glamourize it with shimmering pearlized paint and shells. Add the shell cushion to emphasize the theme.

PAINTING THE CHAIR

Arrange a line or cluster of shells on the chair back, then trim the seat or the chair legs with tiny shells. Small scallop-shaped shells and other flat varieties, interspersed with pearly shells, are ideal.

The chair is painted and decorated like the SHELL MIRROR, so follow the steps for this, using the picture of the chair as a guide for the design.

SCALLOPED CUSHION

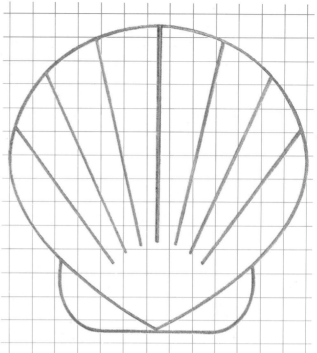

This little cushion will look perfect on your shell-trimmed chair – it's made in the shape of a scallop shell and stitched in shimmery silver thread.

MATERIALS

Two 40cm (15¾in) squares of aqua cotton chintz

One 40cm (15¾in) square of cotton lawn

One 40cm (15¾in) square of lightweight terylene wadding

Silver machine embroidery thread

Terylene toy filling

Dressmakers' carbon paper

Matching sewing thread

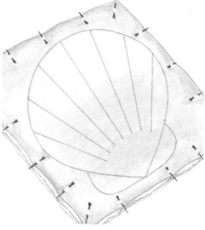

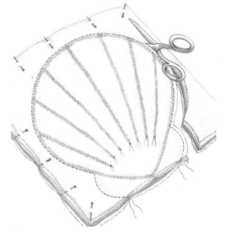

1 PREPARING THE FABRICS
Enlarge the shell pattern on pattern paper and use carbon paper to transfer it on to the right side of one 40cm (15¾in) square of chintz. Sandwich the wadding in between the wrong sides of the marked chintz and the lawn square. Pin the three layers together.

2 QUILTING THE DESIGN
Set the machine to a close zigzag stitch and thread it with the silver thread. Test the tension on a spare piece of fabric and wadding – you may need to loosen the tension for a smooth, even zigzag.

To stitch the scallop design, work over the straight lines and the outline twice with the silver zigzag stitch, then take the thread ends to the wrong side and secure them.

3 ASSEMBLING THE CUSHION
With right sides facing, pin the stitched piece to the second chintz square. Using matching thread, stitch round the outer edge, following the outside edge of the zigzag stitch, and leaving a 10cm (4in) opening at the flat side of the shell. Trim the seam to 6mm (2¼in) and turn the cushion out. Pad it with toy filling, then slipstitch the opening closed.

Marine Theme Bathroom – Window treatments

Complete your aqua bathroom with a pretty window dressing and accessories. Foamy chintz and organza drapes soften the outline of a practical roller blind, and shells, embroidered in silver thread, add a touch of luxury to towels and a bathmat.

▼ **Emphasize the seaside theme by stencilling shell motifs on a plain, ready-made roller blind. The mid aqua motifs show up well on the dark blind.**

SHELL BATHMAT

This witty shell bathmat is made from a large towel and embroidered with silver thread to match the towels and other bathroom accessories.

MATERIALS

A 140 x 66cm (55 x 26in) bath towel

Matching thread and needle

70cm (27½in) square of lightweight polyester wadding

Silver machine embroidery thread

Dressmakers' pattern paper

Air or water dissolvable marker pen

1 TRANSFERRING THE DESIGN
Scale up the pattern, and transfer it on to pattern paper. Centre the pattern on the towel and mark round it with an air or water dissolvable marker pen. Cut it out along the outer line. Prick holes along the design lines and, using the marker pen, mark the pattern clearly through these.

1 square = 5cm (2in)

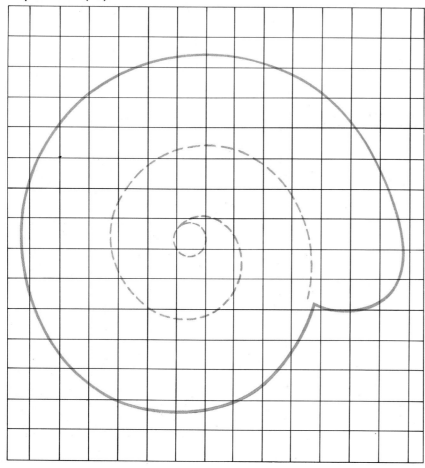

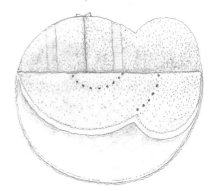

2 MAKING THE MAT
Join the ends of the remaining towel pieces. Cut out a second mat shape from this, and one from wadding. Place the towelling shapes together, right sides facing, then place the wadding over the marked towelling shape. Sew all round with matching thread, taking a 1cm (⅜in) seam, and leaving a 10cm (4in) opening. Turn the mat to the right side and slipstitch the gap closed.

3 STITCHING THE DESIGN
Using a wide machine zigzag stitch and silver thread, work over the dotted lines twice through all layers. Knot the thread ends on the wrong side.

NO-SEW WINDOW DRAPES

It takes just moments to create this frothy window dressing. All you have to do is drape floaty organza and plain chintz over special valance creators – you can buy these in soft furnishing departments. There's no need to hem the fabrics unless they fray very easily.

1 PREPARING THE WINDOW
Screw the valance creators to the wall by the top corners of the window.

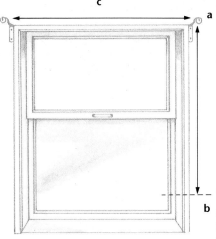

2 CUTTING THE FABRICS
Decide how long the drapes should be. Measure this length (**a** to **b**), double it and add the window width (**c**). Add 1m (1⅛yd) for the 'knots'. Cut this length in both organza and chintz. Trim the chintz to make it a little narrower than the organza.

3 JOINING THE FABRICS
Lay the chintz over the organza with the right side of both fabrics facing downwards, and wrap the edges of the organza over the chintz. Using string, tie the fabrics together in the middle and at each end.

4 HANGING THE DRAPES
Place the fabrics over the valance creators with the centre over the middle of the window. Twist each end through a valance creator, pull the ends into shape and remove the string.

▶ White organza, layered over sea-green chintz, creates a lovely, shimmery window drape. To work out the fabric amounts, see step 2. The white coil is a valance creator.

EMBROIDERED TOWELS

Add a designer touch to your bathroom with these embroidered towels. For really smooth, even stitching, use special craft tracing paper which you stitch over and then tear away, such as Vilene Stitch 'N' Tear.

EMBROIDERING THE MOTIFS
Trace one of the shell motifs (see right) on to the craft paper. Pin it in position on the towel.

Set your machine to a close zigzag stitch, then test the tension on a scrap of towel and fabric – you may need to loosen it. On the towel, work over the design lines twice with machine zigzag stitch, using silver machine embroidery thread. Secure the thread ends on the wrong side. Finish off with a line of satin stitch down the centre of the towel border. Tear off the tracing paper.

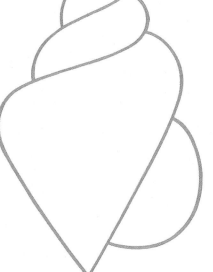

shell templates

STENCILLING A ROLLER BLIND

Stencilling a roller blind is just as easy as stencilling a wall. If your bathroom window is very small, copy the design on the blind in the picture – three marine motifs are stencilled on the hemline in two shades of aqua. If your window is larger, create an all-over design or a bold shell border – the stencilling technique is the same.

MATERIALS

A stiffened roller blind

Light and medium aqua emulsion paint

Small pieces of synthetic sponge

Shell stencils (pages 128-129)

Two plates

Protective sheeting (optional)

Old newspapers

Spray adhesive

Solvent

Masking tape

Pencil

Ruler

Eraser

Hairdryer (optional)

1 PREPARING THE BLIND
Cover the work surface with protective sheeting or old newspapers and lay the blind, right side up, on top Weight the blind to hold it flat. Mask off the areas you don't want to stencil with old newspaper.

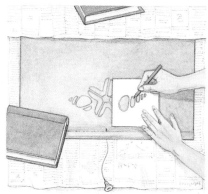

2 POSITIONING THE SHELLS
Mark the centre of the blind just above the hemline. For a small blind, position the starfish stencil centrally just above the line of stitching on the hem. Draw lightly around the starfish with pencil. Mark the positions for two spiral shells in the same way, using the photograph as a guide.

If your blind is larger, plan out your border or all-over design before marking in the stencil positions.

3 ADDING THE FIRST MOTIF
Lightly spray the back of a stencil with adhesive and position it over the pencil outline. Pour some light aqua paint on to a plate and, using an almost dry sponge, dab the paint through the stencil to colour the top half of the motif only. Repeat with the medium aqua paint, but this time colour the lower half of the motif.

If the paint sinks into the fabric, dry it with the hairdryer, then sponge on some more colour.

4 COMPLETING THE DESIGN
Carefully remove the stencil and use a little solvent to wipe away any excess adhesive. When the paint is completely dry, stencil the other motifs in the same way.

Tip

PEARLY STENCILS
If you want the shells on your blind to look pearly to match your shell decorations, wait until the aqua paint has dried, then place the stencil over the shell again and give it a quick spray with silver spray paint.

Cottage Style Bedroom

If you hanker for the rural simplicity of a country house, bring some of its style into your bedroom with pretty coordinated cushions, trimmed sheets and accessories. Recreate this look with fresh blue and white fabrics in traditional prints.

In this room you can make:
- Cross-stitch cushion
- Gingham laundry bag
- Frilled lampshade
- Lined basket
- Café curtains

◀ Stitch a handy laundry bag with a coordinating checked bow and add a designer touch to your bathrobe with striped binding.

▶ Store your make-up in a pretty fabric-lined basket with useful deep side pockets.

The inspiration for this pretty cottage style bedroom is fresh blue and white set against white painted tongue-and-groove panelled walls, simple solid pine furniture and wicker accessories. With a neutral background like this and fabrics in just two colours, you can combine as many patterns as you like without the look becoming too fussy. Here, both broad and narrow stripes are mixed together with cheerful checks and pretty florals in soft shades of blue.

If you're not keen on blue, but you like this room's overall look, you could achieve a similar effect with pink and white or green and white fabrics and plain painted or papered walls. If you find white walls too stark, you could paint them with a tinted white emulsion to complement the fabric colours – there are several shades to choose from. Just remember to keep the background simple and stick to two main colours in your fabrics, teamed with the mellow shades of natural wood furniture.

FLOWER CUSHION

This attractive flower cushion will take pride of place in your bedroom. It's embroidered in cross stitch and stem stitch, and it's finished off with a pretty lace frill around the edge.

MATERIALS

30 x 40cm (12 x 16in) cushion pad

40cm (½yd) of 150cm (60in) wide fine white linen

30 x 40cm (12 x 16in) rectangle of evenweave linen, with 30 threads to 2.5cm (1in)

Blue stranded embroidery cotton (DMC 793 or Anchor 176)

1.8m (2yd) of 4cm (1½in) wide cotton lace trim

Dressmakers' marker pencil

Sharp embroidery needle

2 WORKING THE CROSS STITCH
Tack the evenweave linen centrally on to the large rectangle of linen, taking a 1.5cm (⅝in) seam allowance all round. Use the picture as a guide to place the motifs in the corners, 1.5cm (⅝in) in from the tacking line. Following the chart opposite and using two strands of embroidery cotton, work the flowers in cross stitch over two threads of fabric.

3 FINISHING THE EMBROIDERY
Mark the stems with the dressmakers' marker pencil and, using two strands of cotton, embroider them in stem stitch.

Trim away the evenweave linen around the embroidery and carefully remove the threads, leaving the embroidery on the linen.

1 PREPARING THE PIECES
For the cushion front, cut out a 33 x 43cm (13¼ x 17¼in) rectangle of fine white linen. For the back, cut two 33 x 25cm (13¼ x 10in) rectangles from the linen.

Stitch a double 1cm (⅜in) hem along one long edge of each back rectangle.

GINGHAM LAUNDRY BAG

This handy laundry bag is made from two checked fabrics. It's very pretty, so why not hang it on a hook on the wall to show it off.

MATERIALS

1m (1⅛yd) of 90cm (36in) wide large check fabric

30cm (⅜yd) of 90cm (36in) wide small check fabric

Matching sewing threads

Rouleau turner or safety pin

CUTTING LIST

From large check fabric
- 100 x 75cm (39½ x 29½in) rectangle
- 20 x 7cm (8 x 2¾in) rectangle for the hanging loop

From small check fabric
- Sufficient 15cm (6in) wide strips to make up an 175cm (69in) strip

Note: take 1.5cm (⅝in) seam allowances throughout.

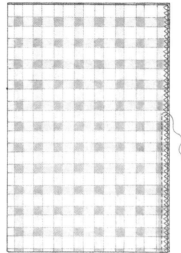

1 SEWING THE BAG
Fold the large rectangle of fabric in half lengthways with the right sides together, and stitch one long edge for 35cm (13¾in). Neaten the raw edges of the seam with machine zigzag stitch. Press the seam open.

2 STITCHING THE BASE
Centre the seam on the front of the bag, then pin and stitch the base edge through both fabric layers. Neaten the seam edges with zigzag stitch.

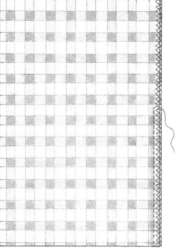

3 MAKING THE TOP CASING
At the top of the bag, turn under 1cm (⅜in), then 8cm (3¼in) to make a double hem. Press the hem, then stitch it along the lower edge.

4 ADDING THE HANGING LOOP
Fold the loop fabric strip in half lengthways, with right sides together. Stitch the long edge, then turn the fabric tube to the right side using the rouleau turner or safety pin. Press the tube.

Stitch one end of the loop to the back of the bag on the top left, stitching through one fabric layer only. Stitch the other end of the loop to the top right edge in the same way.

5 MAKING THE TIE
Fold the long strip of fabric in half lengthways, with right sides facing and stitch the long edge. Turn the tube out and slipstitch the ends closed. Press the tie and thread it through the top casing. Pull it up and tie it in a bow.

◄ Give your bathrobe a designer touch with striped binding. Just make a giant 12cm (4¾in) wide bias strip from striped cotton, and stitch it round the front edges and cuffs. Unpick the pockets and add striped linings, allowing extra fabric to extend to the pocket fronts; re-attach the pockets. You can also cover one side of the belt with a fabric strip.

FRILLED LAMPSHADE

Make this simple, gathered lampshade to match your colour scheme. It's elasticated for an easy fit.

MATERIALS

25cm (10in) empire lampshade frame, 16.5cm (6½in) high

1.2m (1⅜yd) of 90cm (36in) wide cotton fabric

1.3m (1½yd) of 1cm (⅜in) wide ribbon

1.8m (2yd) of cord elastic

Bodkin or safety pin

Matching sewing threads

CUTTING LIST

From cotton fabric
- 90 x 30cm (36 x 12in) rectangle for the cover
- 12cm (4¾in) wide strips of fabric to make up a strip 1.8m (2yd) long

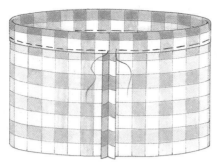

1 JOINING THE COVER
Fold the fabric rectangle in half widthways, with the right sides together and the short edges matching. Stitch the short edges together, taking a 1cm (⅜in) seam. At the top edge, turn 1cm (⅜in) to the wrong side, and then 4cm (1½in) to make a double hem. Press and tack the hem in place. Turn out the cover to the right side.

2 ADDING THE RIBBON TRIM
Taking the seam as the centre back, mark the centre front of the fabric with a pin. Fold the ribbon in half lengthways to find the centre, and pin this over the seam, covering the tacked hem. Pin the ribbon round to the front. Sewing along each edge, machine stitch the ribbon to the cover, leaving a small gap at each side of the centre front so that you can thread the elastic through. Remove the tacking.

TOILETRY BASKET

This basket has a lining with built-in pockets to hold cosmetics and toiletries. The lining fits a wicker basket 20cm (8in) across and 11cm (4½in) deep.

MATERIALS

80cm (⅞yd) of 90cm (36in) wide cotton fabric

80cm (⅞yd) of cord elastic

Matching sewing threads

Bodkin or safety pin

Dressmakers' marker pen

Lightweight wadding

CUTTING LIST

From cotton fabric
- 78 x 24cm (31 x 9½in) rectangle for the main lining
- 78 x 13cm (31 x 5¼in) strip for the pockets
- Two 12cm (4¾in) strips cut across the width of the fabric to make a piece 160cm (63in) long
- Two 23cm (9in) diameter circles

From wadding
- One 23cm (9in) diameter circle

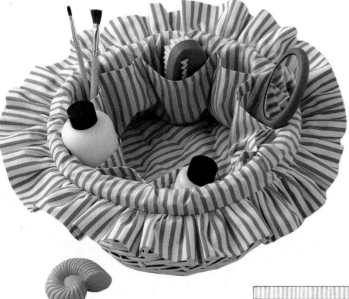

1 MAKING THE LINING
Stitch a 1cm (⅜in) deep hem along the lower edge of the main lining rectangle. Stitch a 1cm (⅜in) hem along the top edge of the pocket strip. Turn 5mm (¼in) to the wrong side along the long raw edge of the pocket strip and press it.

2 STITCHING THE POCKETS
Lay the main lining flat with the right side facing upwards and the long raw edge at the top. Pin the pocket strip on top, right side up, with the hemmed edge 5cm (2in) below the top

of the main lining. Stitch along the lower edge of the pocket strip.

Using the dressmakers' marker pen, mark the centre of the lining. Starting from this point, mark the pocket divisions, then stitch them.

BOW-TRIMMED CAFE CURTAINS

You can create a pretty cottage look at any window by adding sheer, frilled café curtains, trimmed with crisp cotton bows. Make the bows from blue and white fabric scraps left over from your other furnishings and accessories, and then stitch them across the curtain top, mix-and-match style.

Follow the instructions to make a curtain with a double frilled top and casement heading or, if you prefer, you can trim existing café curtains by simply following step 3 to make and attach the bows.

MATERIALS

Sheer fabric (see step 1 for details)

Net rod or narrow diameter curtain pole

Cotton fabric remnants

Matching sewing threads

Safety pin or bodkin

1 CUTTING THE CURTAIN FABRIC
Measure the window and cut out the sheer fabric to make a piece twice the width of the window by the required depth, plus 50cm (19½in) for turnings. Join pieces with French seams where necessary.

2 MAKING THE CURTAIN
Turn a double 2cm (¾in) hem along the lower edge of the curtain fabric and a double 1cm (⅜in) hem along the two sides. At the top edge, fold over 23cm (9in) twice to the right side and tack along the top edge, securing the folds. Measure the pole or rod depth and add 1cm (⅜in). Mark this distance from the top fold on the wrong side of the curtain. Tack across the fabric at this point and then stitch it to make a casing. Remove the tacking.

3 MAKING THE BOWS
Make enough bows to space them at 20cm (8in) intervals across the pole or rod. For each bow, cut out a 34 x 4cm (13½ x 1½in) strip of fabric. Fold the strip in half lengthways with the right sides together. Stitch the long side taking a 6mm (¼in) seam. Turn out the strip, hand stitch the ends closed and tie it into a bow. Work a couple of stitches through the centre to secure the knot. Hand stitch the bows in place along the casing stitching line, making sure you don't stitch right through the casing. Hang the curtain.

▶ Decorate a mini cupboard to match your bedroom. Back the fabric with mediumweight iron-on interfacing, then cut a fabric rectangle to fit the door panel. Using the heart shape on page 89 as a template, cut out the shape in the size you need, then stick the fabrics in place with PVA or craft adhesive.

AN OPULENT THEME

The starting point for this luxurious bedroom is the floral fabric in deep red, chocolate brown and green, with warm golden highlights. It is used to make a soft, quilted bedspread, topped with coordinating pillows, matching coronet drapes and quilted lingerie case.

The bedspread is made by quilting the fabric layers together and then adding a wide border. You can make the border from a 25cm (10in) wide bias strip, the same length as the circumference of the bedspread; pad it with wadding and then apply it like binding. Alternatively, make the border from a 25cm (1in) wide straight-cut strip, twice the circumference of the bedspread; gather it up to fit, pad it with wadding and fold in the long raw edges. Topstitch it to the bedspread. For the finishing touch, you can stitch double piping along the border seam.

The main colours of the fabric are picked out and used elsewhere in the room – the walls are colourwashed in pale beige to create a light background for the stronger colour accents, such as the red and green used on the hand-painted mirror frame. For added grandeur, the gold highlights in the fabric are repeated on the magnificent golden coronet and gilded candle-holder.

If you like, you can create a different, but equally magnificent look by changing the balance of colours in the room scheme – you could colourwash the walls in green or red for a richer look, or add more cream or beige accents for a lighter touch.

◀ The rich red floral fabric (top) is used as the basis of this room scheme. Creamy beige, green and rust red are picked out as accent colours. However, you don't have to use these colours – the blue floral fabric (bottom) would make an equally attractive starting point for a blue colour scheme.

1 QUILTING THE FABRICS

Carefully fuse a Quiltex rectangle to each wadding rectangle. Pin the wadding to the wrong side of the main fabric with the Quiltex on the outside. With the right side of the main fabric downwards, machine stitch across every alternate line on the Quiltex. By drawing round a mug, mark the lower corners of each side panel and the top edge of the main section into curves. Cut round the curves.

2 ADDING THE LINING

Pin the lining pieces to each bag section with the right sides of the fabric together. Machine stitch across one short end of each section. Fold the lining of each section over to the wrong side and press it. Trim the lining to match the curves on the wadding. Tack the layers together 6mm (¼in) from the edges.

3 ASSEMBLING THE CASE

With the linings together and the stitched edges level, pin and tack a side panel to each long edge of the main piece along the tacking lines.

Turn under one end of the binding. With this end at the straight edge of the bag, stitch one long edge of the binding to one seam of the bag, with the right sides together. When you reach the end of the seam, trim the end of the binding and turn down the end to neaten it. Press under the free long edge of the binding and slipstitch it to the other side of the seam, enclosing the raw edges.

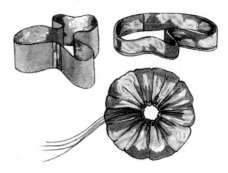

4 MAKING THE ROSETTES

Stitch the short edges of each strip together, with the right sides of the fabric facing, to make a loop. Press the seam open, then press the strip in half, with the wrong sides together. Work two rows of gathering threads along the raw edges, and pull them up tightly to form a rosette. Secure the gathers at the centre with a few stitches.

5 ATTACHING THE FASTENINGS

Fold the flap of the case over. Stitch two hooks, 19cm (7½in) apart, under the flap, then sew the corresponding eyes to the bag front. Pin the rosettes over the hooks and eyes, placing a button in the centre of each rosette to cover the raw edges. Stitch through the button shank to secure the button and rosette.

COLOURWASHING

Colourwashing creates a greater depth of colour than plain, painted walls, and it's one of the easiest paint techniques.

To create the look in the picture (below), paint the walls with two coats of buttermilk matt emulsion and leave the paint to dry. In a bucket, mix one part of pale beige matt emulsion with four parts of water. Using a large brush, apply this diluted paint to the wall, over an area of about 1m (1yd) square at a time.

Rinse the brush, and, while it is still damp, wipe it over the paint to blur the brushmarks. After a few minutes, firmly brush over the paint again to remove some of the paint. This creates a soft, patchy effect. Soften any remaining brushmarks by dabbing over them with a sponge.

▼ Colourwashing gives a very subtle effect and is a simple look to achieve. The pale beige colourwash used here is a perfect background for the rich fabrics and gilded accessories in this classical look bedroom.

PAINTED MIRROR FRAME

This elegant mirror started out as a plain Thai silk photo frame, but you could make your own frame from fabric-covered card. The swirly design is coloured to coordinate with the bedroom furnishings.

When you are buying your fabric paints, take a sample of your main fabric with you to help you to match up the colours.

You can get mirrors cut to specific measurements in DIY stores.

MATERIALS

Cream fabric-covered frame with a border about 5cm (2in) deep

Mirror, cut to fit the frame

Fabric paints in deep dusky pink, deep pink, white and green

Gold marker pen

Selection of artists' brushes

Dressmakers' marker pen

Tracing paper and transfer pencil

Bowls/saucers for mixing the paints

Decorative furnishing cord, sufficient to wrap twice round the frame plus 30cm (12in)

Matching sewing thread

Small, sharp needle

Clear craft adhesive

1 PAINTING THE BACKGROUND
In the bowls or saucers, mix three shades of dusky pink fabric paint – light, medium and dark – to tone with your fabric. Using a large artists' brush, paint the whole frame light pink. Using medium pink, paint a border about 1cm (⅜in) deep along the inner edge.

2 PAINTING THE OUTER BORDER
Using the dressmakers' marker pen, mark the centre of the side and lower edges of the frame, 2.5cm (1in) in from the outer edges. Mark the top centre point, 2cm (1½in) in from the edge.

Using medium pink, paint a border about 1.5cm (⅝in) deep around the outer edges of the frame, sweeping the inner edge of the border in to meet the marks, and curving the corners.

3 ADDING THE DEEP PINK LINES
Using deep pink and a fine artists' brush, paint a narrow line around the inner and outer edges of the frame. Then use deep pink to outline the curved edge of the medium pink outer border.

4 TRANSFERRING THE DESIGN
Using the tracing paper and transfer pencil, copy the design elements from the pattern on the next page on to the frame, lining them up with the centre points. You will probably need to adjust the pattern slightly to fit your frame.

5 PAINTING THE DESIGN
Using a fine brush, paint the leaves in green and add deep pink highlights. Then use the gold pen to draw in the swirls and outline the leaves. Outline the edges of the inner deep pink border in gold. Finally, highlight the deep pink edging of the outer border in gold.

6 PREPARING THE CORD TRIM
Seal the ends of the cord with a little adhesive and leave it to dry. Fold the cord in half.

FLANGED PILLOWCASE

A smart flanged pillowcase looks especially good on a large, square continental pillow. But you can also copy this idea to make covers for standard pillows and cushions.

MATERIALS

65cm (25½in) square continental pillow

1m (1¼yd) of sheeting

Matching sewing threads

Dressmakers' pins

CUTTING LIST

From sheeting
- One 68 x 22cm (26¾ x 8¾in) rectangle for the pillow flap
- One 68cm (26¾in) square for the back
- One 80cm (31½in) square for the front

1 STITCHING THE HEMS
On one long edge of the flap, turn 5mm (¼in) and then 1cm (½in) to the wrong side to make a hem. Pin and machine stitch the hem in place. In the same way, stitch a hem along one edge of the back piece.

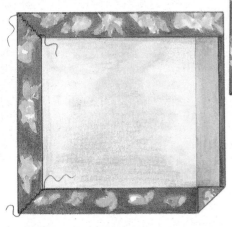

2 MAKING THE FLANGE
On the front piece, press 5mm (¼in) and then 5cm (2in) to the wrong side all round. Fold neat mitres at the corners and trim off the excess fabric. Slipstitch the mitred corners, making sure that the stitches don't go through to the right side where they will show.

3 ATTACHING THE FLAP
With the wrong sides of the fabric together, slip the three raw edges of the flap under the flange at one edge of the front piece; the short edges should almost meet the outer edges of the front piece, but the long edge should only slip under the flange by 1cm (½in). Pin, then slipstitch the long edge of the flap where it meets the flange.

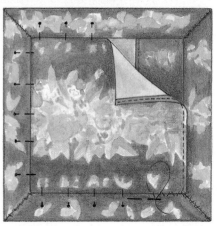

4 ATTACHING THE BACK
With the wrong sides of the fabric together, place the back piece over the front piece and slip the three raw edges under the flange. The stitched hem of the back piece should just overlap the flange at the flap end. Pin and slipstitch the back in place.

5 FINISHING OFF
Working from the back of the pillowcase, machine stitch all round, 3mm (⅛in) from the inside edge of the flange; make sure you don't catch the back opening as you stitch.

THE LOOK

Deep, cool blue and pale butter yellow is a well-loved colour combination. It gives this bedroom traditional appeal, with a fresh, light feel that's typical of the American Country look.

To create the same comfortable scheme in your own bedroom, paint the walls pale yellow, choose a deep blue carpet or rug, and add solid pine furniture and hand-crafted accessories.

If you would prefer a different colour scheme, try yellow walls with rich green, aubergine or deep raspberry pink stripes and checks.

Make your bed the focal point with mix-and-match covers and piles of cushions. To give your bed an impressive four-poster look, hang floor-length drapes behind it from a wooden curtain pole.

PAPER SHADE

This lampshade has a cut-out bird and cherry design. The three-dimensional effect is created by curling the cut flaps.

MATERIALS

36cm (14in) diameter lampshade ring for the base

12.5cm (5in) diameter gimbal lampshade ring for the top

76 x 56cm (30 x 22in) sheet of watercolour paper (standard size)

Tracing paper

Roll of white crêpe paper

Greaseproof paper

1.8m (2yd) bias binding

Small craft knife

3mm (¹⁄₁₆in) wad punch or tapestry needle and a knitting needle

Protective cutting surface

Scissors, pencil and eraser

Paperclips

PVA craft adhesive

Stick adhesive

LAMPSHADE PATTERN
1 square = 2.5cm (1in)

CONTRAST-BORDER CURTAINS

These unlined white curtains have decorative striped borders all the way round and matching ties.

MATERIALS

White cotton fabric

Blue and white striped cotton fabric for the borders and ties

Tape measure, scissors and pins

Matching sewing threads

CUTTING LIST

*Decide on the finished length of the curtains (**a**), then calculate the finished width of each curtain (**b**).*

From white cotton fabric
- Two rectangles the finished length (**a**) of each curtain by the finished width (**b**)

From contrast fabric
- Two 13cm (5¼in) wide strips the width of each curtain (**b**) for the lower borders
- Four 13cm (5¼in) wide strips the length of each curtain (**a**) plus 1.5cm (⅝in) for the side borders
- Four 8cm (3¼in) wide strips the width of each curtain (**b**) plus 3cm (1¼in) for the top borders
- 32 x 12cm (12½ x 4¾in) strips for the ties: enough to place a pair at each end and other pairs at about 18cm (7in) intervals in between

Note: Join strips for the borders as necessary, taking 1cm (⅜in) seams. Otherwise take 1.5cm (⅝in) seams throughout.

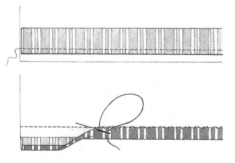

1 ADDING THE LOWER BORDERS

With the right sides together, pin one long raw edge of the lower border on the lower edge of the curtain, 3.5cm (1⅜in) up from the raw edge. Stitch 1.5cm (⅝in) up from the edge of the border. Press the seam, then press 1.5cm (⅝in) to the wrong side on the other long border edge. Fold the border over the edge of the curtain, enclosing the seam, and press it: the finished border is 5cm (2in) wide. Slipstitch the turned edge on the wrong side of the curtain.

2 ADDING THE SIDE BORDERS

Stitch a side border along each long edge of the curtain in the same way as the lower border, but position it so that it overhangs the lower edge of the curtain by 1.5cm (⅝in). Turn in the overhang and slipstitch it in place.

3 STITCHING THE TIES

With the right sides together, fold each tie in half lengthways. Stitch 1cm (⅜in) in from the edges along one short edge and the long raw edge. Trim the seam allowances at the corners, turn each tie out and press it.

4 ATTACHING THE TIES

On the right side of one top border strip, insert a pin 1.5cm (⅝in) from each short end, and at about 18cm (7in) intervals in between. With the raw edges matching, pin two ties at each pin mark. Tack them 1cm (⅜in) from the raw edge of the border.

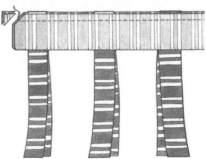

5 FINISHING THE TOP BORDER

With the right sides together, place the second border strip on top of the strip with the ties and stitch 1cm (⅜in) from the long top edge. Trim the seam allowances at the corners.

6 ATTACHING THE TOP BORDER

With the right sides together, pin and stitch one long top border edge 3.5cm (1⅜in) down from the top of the curtain. Press the seam, then turn the border to the wrong side of the curtain. Turn under the raw edges. Slipstitch the border in place on the wrong side of the curtain and at the sides.

DRESSING TABLE AND STOOL COVERS

Make pretty matching covers for your dressing table and stool from two coordinating blue and white fabrics. Follow the steps below to make a stool cover with a soft gathered skirt, trimmed with piping.

MATERIALS

Circular box cushion pad or block foam to fit the stool

Blue and white checked fabric for the cushion (see the CUTTING LIST for the amount)

Blue and white striped fabric for the skirt (see the CUTTING LIST for the amount)

Piping cord

Matching sewing threads

Tape measure and scissors

CUTTING LIST

Place the cushion pad or block foam pad on the stool before you measure up

From blue and white check
- One circle the diameter of the cushion pad (**a**) plus 3cm (1¼in), for the stool top
- One bias strip the measurement around the cushion pad (**b**) plus 3cm (1¼in), by the depth of the cushion pad (**c**) plus 3cm (1¼in) for the side band

From piping cord
- Two lengths the measurement around the cushion pad (**b**), plus 3cm (1¼in)

From blue and white stripe
- Sufficient bias strips to cover the cord
- For the skirt, sufficient widths of fabric the height of the stool from the floor to the cushion base (**d**) plus 4.5cm (1¾in) to make a piece 1½-2½ times the measurement around the cushion pad (**b**)

Note: Take 1.5cm (⅝in) seams throughout

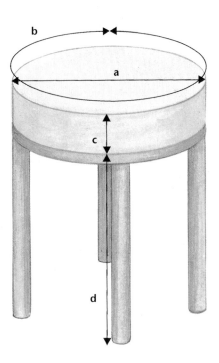

GLASS TOPS
Tip

A glass top will protect your dressing table and provide a wipe-clean surface. Take your paper pattern to your glass supplier – you may need to adjust the pattern so that the glass will sit neatly inside the piped edging of the top cover.

◄ Pretty, hand-painted blue glass containers will complement the colour scheme in your American Country bedroom. Simply buy inexpensive blue glass containers and paint on yellow flower shapes and dots. Use special glass paint and a fine artists' watercolour brush, available from art and craft shops.

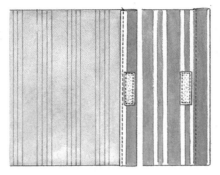

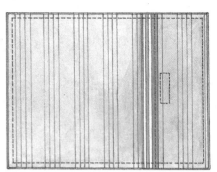

2 MAKING THE ZIGZAG EDGING
Lay the cushion front out flat with the right side facing up. With the raw edges of the fabric matching, place one triangle at one end of a short side, with the single fold towards the corner. Place a second triangle next to this, overlapping the first one slightly, and with the folded edge facing in the same direction. Add three more triangles in this way. Stitch the triangles in place, 1cm (⅜in) from the raw edge. Repeat for the other side.

3 ADDING THE FASTENINGS
Fold and press a double 2cm (¾in) hem along one short end of the cushion back. Stitch the hem. Pin, then stitch one half of the touch-and-close tape centrally over the wrong side of the hem.

Press under a double 2cm (¾in) hem along one long edge of the flap strip. Stitch the hem. Pin, then stitch the other part of the tape centrally on the right side of the hem, 2.5cm (1in) from the hem edge.

4 ASSEMBLING THE CUSHION
Place the cushion back over the cushion front with the right sides of the fabric together and three raw edges matching. Place the flap on top, with the wrong side of the fabric facing upwards, and with the long raw edge matching the fourth edge of the cushion front. Stitch all round the cushion, 1cm (⅜in) from the raw edges. Trim the seam allowances at the corners, then neaten them.

BOW-TRIMMED CUSHIONS

MATERIALS

40 x 35cm (15¾ x 13¾in) cushion pad

Two 43 x 38cm (17 x 15in) rectangles of blue and white checked fabric for the back and front

Four 38 x 8cm (15 x 3¼in) strips of blue and white checked fabric for the front and back facings

Twelve 34 x 8cm (13½ x 3¼in) strips of blue and white striped fabric for the ties

160cm (59in) length of piping cord, covered in blue and white striped bias strips

Matching sewing threads

Dressmakers' marker pen

Tape measure

1 STITCHING THE PIPING
Pin, then stitch the covered piping to the right side of one checked rectangle, stitching it 1.5cm (⅝in) from the edges.

2 ATTACHING THE TIES
Fold each tie in half with the right sides together. Stitch the long edge and one short end. Clip the corners, turn each tie right side out and press it.

Lay the piped cushion front flat, with the right side up. Pin three ties along each short side seam with the raw edges matching. Space them evenly, with each end strip close to a corner seamline. Pin the remaining ties on the other rectangle, making sure that the ties match up with the cushion front. Stitch the ties in place, 1.5cm (⅝in) from the raw edges.

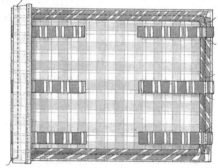

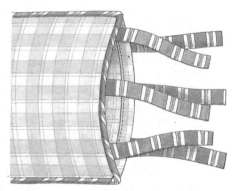

3 ATTACHING THE FACINGS
Stitch a 1cm (⅜in) double hem along one long edge of each facing strip. Place a strip over the ties on the front and back pieces, with the raw edges matching. Stitch a 1.5cm (⅝in) seam. Trim the seam allowances, turn out the facings and press them.

4 FINISHING OFF
Pin the front and back right sides together and tack along the two long edges and the ends of the facing bands. Stitch along the seams, then remove the tacking. Turn out the cover, insert the cushion pad and knot the ties in pretty bows across the openings.

BORDERED BED DRAPES

Make an eye-catching feature of your bed with lavish bed drapes, made to match your window curtains. You don't have to have a four-poster bed to create this effect – you could drape a length of your curtain fabric from a painted wooden pole fixed above the bedhead, or put up a half-tester fitting or a coronet with curtains and a matching valance.

MAKING THE DRAPES

Hang your bed drapes from a track, just like curtains, or attach them to eye hooks positioned along the bed frame, coronet or half-tester.

Make your full-length bed drapes with smart contrasting borders to match the curtains, but omit the top ties, and use standard curtain tape and curtain hooks instead.

Make the valance frill in the same way as the drapes, but omit the side borders. The valance should be 30-50cm (12-20in) deep. You can make a valance for a four-poster bed in separate sections to accommodate corners, or in one long strip to go all the way round. On a coronet, the valance will go all the way round the curved outer edge.

MINI-PRINT PICTURES

Cover ready-made card picture mounts with coordinating fabrics to complement your favourite pictures. These mounts look particularly effective with pictures which have large, plain background areas because they help to balance the pictures.

For a really smart effect, use a double picture mount – this is made by laying one picture mount on top of another mount in a different colour or pattern. The top, outer mount has a larger window, so that you can see the inner edges of the under mount. You can make your own double picture mount or combine ready-made ones bought from a frame shop or an art and craft shop.

For the covers, choose two coordinating mini-print fabrics, as larger patterns may overpower the picture. Use the darker fabric for the under mount (the one placed next to the picture) and the lighter fabric for the top, outer mount.

PADDED SHAKER BOX

This padded Shaker style box is perfect for storing jewellery and other small accessories. It's a no-sew project and you can choose colours to suit your bedroom.

MATERIALS

25 x 18.5cm (10 x 7¼in) Shaker style box

50cm (⅝yd) of printed cotton

Toning braid, ribbon or fabric to trim the lid

50cm (⅝yd) of mediumweight wadding

Sheet of firm card

PVA fabric adhesive

Fray preventer

Scissors

Tape measure

Pencil

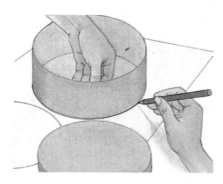

1 CUTTING THE CARD
Lay the box base and lid on the card and draw round them. Cut out the two ovals, then trim away 6mm (¼in) all round each shape. Check the fit inside the box and lid; the card should fit loosely to allow for the thickness of the fabric and wadding. Measure around the inside of the box, then measure the depth; cut a strip of card to these measurements, and trim about 6mm (¼in) from one short edge.

2 ADDING THE WADDING
Lay the three card shapes on the wadding and draw around them. Cut along the marked lines. Using the PVA fabric adhesive, glue each wadding shape on to the matching card shape.

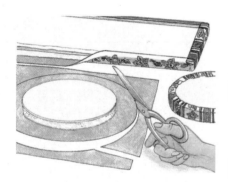

3 COVERING THE CARD
Lay the fabric out flat with the wrong side facing upwards. Lay the wadded card shapes on top, with the wadding facing downwards; take note of any pattern directions. Draw around each shape, 5cm (2in) from the edges, and cut along the marked lines. Spread a line of adhesive round the edges of the card and, gathering the fabrics slightly at the curves, press the overlaps on to this to stick them down. Leave the glue to dry.

4 ADDING THE PADDED LININGS
Spread adhesive on the card side of the base and lid linings and press them into place. Leave the glue to dry. Spread adhesive on the inner edges of the box, right up to the rim, and press the padded side section in place. Butt-join the ends and hold them in place while the glue dries.

5 TRIMMING THE LID
To trim the lid with braid or ribbon, measure around the outside of the lid and add 1cm (⅜in) for an overlap. Cut a length of braid to this size and glue it in place, tucking under the raw end that lies on top.

To trim the lid with fabric, measure as before and add 1cm (⅜in). Cut a strip of fabric to this measurement, coat it with fray preventer, then glue it in place as for the braid or ribbon.

▲ **The padded lining inside this wooden Shaker-style box makes it perfect for storing delicate items, such as jewellery. Alternatively you could use it to hold a few sewing implements, such as needles, threads and scissors.**

DECORATING A BABY'S ROOM

This nursery shows how a baby's room can be both charming and functional. Once you've sorted out the essentials – a sturdy cot and storage space – you can concentrate on creating the look.

The starting point is soft white, which is used for walls, woodwork and the floor. The effect is light, unfussy and spacious, and it creates a perfect background for delicate pastel furnishings and accessories. White is a particularly good choice as it can be combined with any colour – here soft pink was used to set a traditional theme for a baby girl but pale blue would work just as well.

Whichever accent colours you use in the white nursery – pink, pale blue, green or lemon – include some fabric prints which use both your accent colour and white. This will help to bring the whole scheme together.

◄ **Lemon, blue, green or pink all make good accent colours for a white nursery, provided the fabrics also include some white. If you don't know whether the baby's going to be a boy or a girl, go for a combination of colours.**

HANGING COT TIDY

Hang this space-saving accessory at the end of a cot or inside a cupboard door. The pockets will hold tiny clothes, small items of nursery equipment and a few small toys. The finished cot tidy is about 50 x 58cm (19¾ x 23in).

MATERIALS

1m (1⅛yd) of 120cm (48in) wide flowery fabric

60cm (¾yd) of 120cm (48in) wide flower and stripe fabric

2.4m (2¾yd) of 1.5cm (⅝in) wide pink satin bias binding

3m (3¼yd) of 2.5cm (1in) wide pink ribbon

Matching sewing threads

CUTTING LIST

Follow the diagram and cut out:

From flowery fabric

- Two 17.5 x 82.5cm (6⅞ x 31¾in) rectangles for the top pockets A to D (made in one section)
- Four 20.5 x 21.5cm (8⅛ x 8½in) rectangles for pockets E and F
- Two 19 x 66.5cm (7½ x 26in) rectangles for pockets G and H (made in one section)
- One 50.5 x 60cm (20 x 23¾in) rectangle for the backing

From flower and stripe print fabric

- One 21.5 x 25cm (8½in x 10in) rectangle for the centre panel
- One 51 x 59.5cm (20 x 23½in) rectangle for the back lining

Note: 1cm (⅜in) seam allowances are included on all pieces where necessary.

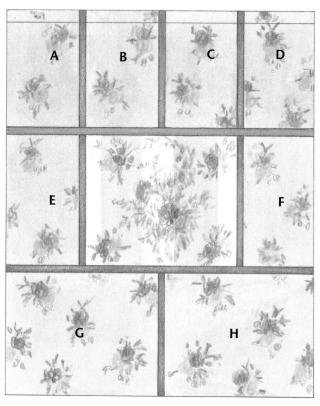

FLOUNCED BLIND

A flounced blind is really just a single curtain divided into flounced panels by vertical tapes and cords. The top is gathered up with standard curtain heading tape and hooked on to a curtain track, just like an ordinary curtain.

You'll need eye hooks to thread the cords through at the top of the blind. If your curtain track is already fixed to a wooden batten, screw the eye hooks into this. Otherwise, screw them into the window frame or a wooden batten fixed below the track.

The diagram (right) shows the reverse side of the flounced blind, so that you can see how it's made. It will also be a helpful guide when you're adding the curtain tape, rings and cords in steps 5 and 6. The area of fullness between the vertical tapes is the *flounce*. Flounces are usually about 46cm (18in) wide, but you can vary this to fit your window.

The cords pass through the rings on the vertical tape, then through the eye hooks fitted under the curtain track and across to one side of the window where they are held together to form a *pull cord*. Use the pull cord to raise or lower the blind, securing it to a cleat fitted beside the window.

MATERIALS

Fabric (see step 2 for amount)

Curtain heading tape and hooks

Narrow webbing tape and fine picture cord (see step 3 for amounts)

Small curtain rings

Eye hooks (one per line of tape)

Cleat and acorn fitting

Matching threads

Dressmakers' marker pen

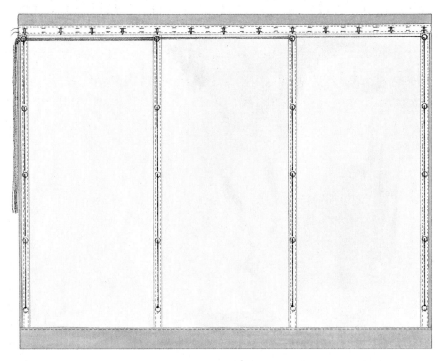

1 PREPARING THE WINDOW
If necessary, fix a wooden batten just below the curtain track. Screw the cleat to the side of the window frame, where it will be easy to reach.

2 MEASURING UP
Measure the track, and allow for fabric at least 1½ times this width. For a full effect and for lightweight fabrics, use twice the track width. Measure the required drop, and add an extra 46cm (18in) for turnings.

3 ESTIMATING TAPES AND CORDS
Cut each tape to the same measurement as the blind drop.

For each cord you will need 1½ times the drop, plus the distance from the top of the tape to the corner of the blind nearest the cleat.

4 MAKING THE BLIND
Join fabric widths if necessary and neaten seams – for a neat finish use French seams.

Press 6.5cm (2½in) to the wrong side along the side edges, and tack them flat. At each side edge, pin tape over the raw edges of the turnings. Machine stitch along each side of the tape. Mark the positions for the other tapes with the marker pen and stitch them in place.

5 THE HEM AND CURTAIN TAPE
Turn up 7.5cm (3in) along the bottom edge for a hem. Turn in 1cm (⅜in) of the hem to neaten the edge and machine stitch across it. At the top edge, turn 7.5cm (3in) to the wrong side and stitch on the curtain heading tape to cover the raw edge.

6 ADDING RINGS AND CORDS
Starting 10cm (4in) from the base hem on one side of the blind, stitch curtain rings to the tape at 25cm (10in) intervals, adding a final ring level with the base of the heading tape. Stitch rings to the other tapes in line with these rings. Securely knot a cord to each base ring and thread it up through the rings to the top.

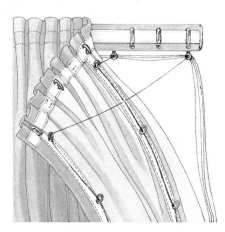

7 HANGING THE BLIND
Fit hooks into the heading tape and gather it up to fit the track. Hang the curtain on the track. Screw an eye hook into the batten in line with each vertical tape, and pass the corresponding cord through each eye. Thread each cord across the top of the blind through all the eyes in the direction of the cleat, and knot them together at one side. Thread the ends of the cord through an acorn fitting and trim them level.

PAINTED ROSES

Painting this ring of roses on to furniture is easy – you simply trace off the design with carbon paper, transfer it on to the furniture and then fill in the carbon outlines with glossy enamel paint.

Enamel paint is an ideal choice – it's brightly coloured, durable and easy to use – any mistakes can be wiped off with a cloth dipped in white spirit, even after the paint has dried. It's sold by hobby and craft shops and stationers, and comes in tiny tins, so it doesn't cost much to buy a range of colours.

If you like, you can paint the rose motif on to other items, such as a cot, a chest of drawers or a toy box. Or you could use just part of the design, such as a single flower, to decorate a small item, such as a lamp base.

ring of roses
trace pattern

BRUSH AND COMB SET

A baby's brush and comb, presented in its own little tray, makes a charming gift for a new arrival.

PAINTING THE BRUSH

The brush is decorated with a single rose, coloured in enamel paints. If there's space on the comb, you could paint that too.

Transfer one rose motif on to the brush with carbon paper and paint it in with enamel paints (see PAINTING THE CHAIR, opposite). Then finish the decoration with a few small green leaves, painted freehand with one quick sweep of the brush.

MAKING THE TRAY

The finished tray is 18.5 x 11cm (7¼ x 4¼in). Seam allowances of 6mm (¼in) are included.

MATERIALS

Two 27 x 20cm (10¾ x 8in) rectangles of cotton fabric (one patterned and one plain)

One 27 x 20cm (10¾ x 8in) rectangle of heavyweight interfacing (craft Vilene)

1.5m (1⅝yd) of 1.5mm (¹⁄₁₆in) wide ribbon in three colours

Matching sewing threads

1 ASSEMBLING THE FABRICS
Place the fabric rectangles together with right sides facing. Lay the interfacing on top and stitch round, leaving a gap to turn the fabric out. Trim the seam allowances across the corners to reduce bulk, then turn the fabrics right sides out and slipstitch the gap closed.

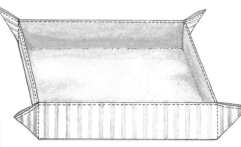

2 SHAPING THE TRAY
Topstitch round the rectangle, as close to the edge as possible. To shape the sides, pinch each corner together so that the top edges are level. Pin in a vertical line down to the base to hold the shape, then tack along this line. Machine stitch along the tacking line. Remove the tacking stitches.

3 ADDING THE RIBBONS
Cut the ribbons into four equal lengths. Arrange them in groups of three colours, and tie each group into a neat bow, sewing firmly through the knot. Stitch a bow to each corner of the tray to finish.

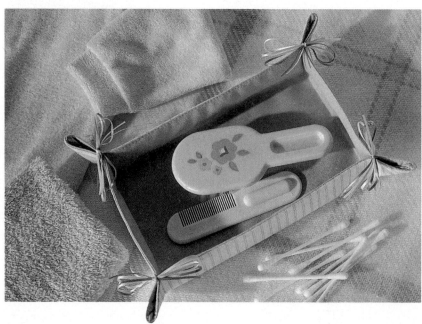

PHOTO ALBUM

A photo album, covered with pretty fabric and embroidered with the baby's name, makes an ideal gift and an attractive keepsake.

This slip-on cover fits a photo album 25 x 26cm (10 x 10¼in), with a 4cm (1½in) wide spine. If your album is a different size, simply cut the fabric 2cm (¾in) deeper than the height of the book, and 20cm (8in) wider than its width across the front, spine and back.

MATERIALS

Photo album 25 x 26cm (10 x 10¼in) with a 4cm (1½in) spine

Two 27 x 76cm (10¾ x 30in) rectangles of cotton fabric, one patterned and one plain

30cm (12in) of 4.5cm (1¾in) wide Aida tape with 15 thread blocks to 2.5cm (1in)

DMC stranded embroidery cotton (see the key for colours)

1 WORKING THE BORDER
Following the chart, and leaving three thread blocks between each letter, stitch the name along the centre of the Aida tape, with motifs at each side. Work each cross stitch over one block of threads.

KEY

◉	Red 666
▨	Pink 996/3326
▫	Green 988
◩	Light green 966
⊠	Yellow green 772

2 MAKING THE COVER
Slipstitch the embroidered tape to the patterned fabric, about 28cm (11in) from the short right edge.

With right sides facing, stitch the patterned and plain fabrics together round the edge, taking 1cm (⅜in) seams, and leaving a small gap to turn the fabric out. Trim the seam allowances at the corners, turn the fabric right sides out and slipstitch the gap closed. Press the cover with a medium hot iron.

3 FITTING THE COVER
Fold each short edge to the plain side by 9cm (3½in) and pin it. Secure the folds at the top and bottom edges with neat slipstitches, using two strands of embroidery cotton. Slip the album into its cover.

FABRIC TEDDY

Make this cute teddy bear from fabric remnants – it couldn't be easier. He's got felt circles for eyes, and his mouth and nose are embroidered. For an even easier face, use safety toy eyes and draw on his nose and mouth in dark fabric pen.

MATERIALS

30cm (¼yd) of 90cm (36in) wide cotton fabric

Matching sewing thread

Scraps of dark felt for the eyes, or two toy eyes

Pale embroidery cotton to highlight the eyes

Pink embroidery cotton for the nose and mouth

60cm (⅜yd) of narrow ribbon

Polyester stuffing

Needle

Scissors

Tracing paper and pencil

Dressmakers' pencil

TEDDY PATTERN

1sq = 2cm

body
cut 2

ear
cut 4

1 CUTTING OUT THE PIECES
Enlarge the pattern pieces for the teddy from the diagram. One square on the chart represents 2cm (¾in). Trace the body twice on to the wrong side of the fabric. If you are using patterned fabric, position the front pattern piece carefully so that the design will look good on the front of the bear.

Trace the eyes, nose and mouth on to the right side of the front bear, then cut out both bear pieces.

Trace the ear four times on to the wrong side of the fabric, then cut them out.

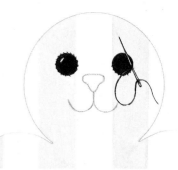

2 ADDING THE EYES
Cut two small felt circles and stitch them on to the bear's face with tiny stitches. If you wish, use blanket stitch. To add a glint to the eyes, use pale embroidery thread to make one small stitch near the top of each eye. Alternatively, fit two toy eyes.

BABY'S QUILT

This delightful baby's quilt is made from three coordinating fabrics – a dainty floral and a plain pink for the patches, with a striped fabric for the border and backing. Padded with wadding, the layers are held together with bows. It measures 105 x 85cm (41½ x 33½in).

MATERIALS

60cm (¾yd) of 137cm (54in) wide printed cotton

60cm (¾yd) of 137cm (54in) wide plain cotton fabric

1.5m (1¾yd) of 137cm (54in) wide striped cotton fabric

1.1m (1¼yd) of 90cm (36in) wide 226g (8oz) polyester wadding

3.5m (3¾yd) of very narrow ribbon in three colours

CUTTING LIST

Cut out the following:
From printed cotton
- Four 22cm (8¾in) squares
- One 37 x 57cm (14½in x 22½in) rectangle cut lengthways

From plain cotton fabric
- Two 37 x 22cm (14½ x 8¾in) rectangles
- Two 57 x 22cm (22½ x 8¾in) rectangles

From striped cotton fabric
- One 77 x 97cm (30½ x 38¼in) rectangle for the backing
- Two 97 x 12cm (38¼ x 4¾in) side strips. Cut these so that the stripes run across the strips.
- Two 87 x 12cm (34¼ x 4¾in) end strips. Cut these so that stripes run across the strips.

From wadding
- One 105 x 85cm (41½ x 33½in) rectangle

Note: a 1cm (⅜in) seam allowance is included on all pieces. Stitch all pieces together with right sides facing.

1 STITCHING THE SIDE PANELS
Pin, then stitch a printed square to each short edge of the 57cm (22½in) long plain rectangles. Make sure that the pattern will run vertically on these side panels. Press the seam allowances open.

2 STITCHING THE CENTRE PANEL
Pin, then stitch a 37cm (14½in) plain rectangle to each short edge of the printed rectangle. Press the seam allowances open.

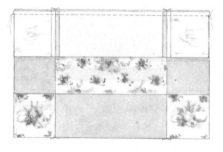

3 JOINING THE PANELS
Matching the seamlines, pin and then stitch a side panel to each side of the centre panel. Press the seam allowances open.

4 ASSEMBLING THE QUILT
Centre the quilt front, right side up, on the wadding, and pin the layers together. Turn the wadding over and centre the striped lining on this side of the wadding, right side up. Tack all three layers together.

5 ADDING THE SIDE STRIPS
Pin, then stitch a 97cm (38¼in) striped strip to each side edge of the quilt front. Match the raw edges of the front and the strips, not the wadding, which will extend beyond the front. Press the seam allowances towards the strips. Fold each strip over the edge of the wadding to the back, tuck the raw edge under, and slipstitch it in place, close to the previous stitching line.

6 ADDING THE END STRIPS
Pin and then stitch an 87cm (34¼in) strip to each short end of the quilt front. Match the raw edges of the front and the strips, but not the wadding, which will extend beyond the front. Fold each strip to the back, tuck in the raw edges on the ends and the long edges and slipstitch them closed.

7 ADDING THE RIBBON BOWS
Using a tapestry needle, thread one colour of fine ribbon through the quilt where the fabrics join, and bring it back up to the front. Thread two more coloured ribbons through at the same point. Tie a small bow with all three ribbons and trim the ends. Repeat to make 15 more bows at the fabric joins.

CREATING THE LOOK

Children love bright, clashing colours and bold motifs, so they'll be delighted with this spirited room scheme. It's based around two coordinating fabrics with bold, bright colours and patterns. Choose fabrics in your child's favourite colours, making sure one of the fabrics has large, simple motifs which you can appliqué on to a plain blanket to create the bedcover. You can also cut out different sections of the fabrics to make coordinating patchwork cushion covers.

Repeat the colours of the fabrics on other items in the room for a coordinated look. You could paint a simple border on the walls, for example, and stick bright motifs on to the furniture, like the brightly painted toy box in the picture. For fun, add colourful bobbles, tassels and braids with a Mexican feel, and decorate small items, like pencil pots and storage boxes, with glittering stick-on jewels.

APPLIQUED BEDCOVER

It takes only a couple of hours to create this colourful bedcover – it's just a plain blanket decorated with motifs cut from fabric.

MATERIALS

Plain single blanket

Fabric with large, bold motifs

Fusible webbing (Bondaweb)

Bright cotton perlé embroidery thread or three to six strands of stranded embroidery cotton – use more strands for thick fabric

Darning needle

Sharp, pointed scissors

An iron

1 ATTACHING THE MOTIFS
Cut out six motifs with a 1.5cm (⅝in) border of fabric around each one. Following the manufacturer's instructions, bond fusible webbing to the back of each motif. Trim the motifs along their outlines and arrange them on the blanket as shown in the diagram (left). Peel off the backing on the fusible webbing and fuse each motif in position on the blanket.

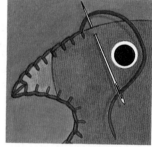

2 STITCHING THE MOTIFS
Using the embroidery thread and the darning needle, blanket stitch around each motif. At the corners, work two or three stitches from the same point for a neat finish.

◄The bright motifs from the fabric stand out beautifully against the strong blue colour of this blanket. Red blanket stitch round the motifs is the finishing touch.

◄ A colourful toy box decorated with stick-on cactus motifs looks great in this child's room and provides lots of storage space.

To copy this idea, start by painting the box or trunk in three or four bright colours. Trace the cactus motifs (below) on to the wrong side of some bright sticky-backed plastic, cut out the shapes and stick them on to the sides and front of the toy box. Use sticky-backed plastic in lots of different colours for a really bright effect.

CACTUS TEMPLATES

HANGING SHELVES

These bright hanging shelves are ideal for storing lightweight items such as paperback books and soft toys. Either use the colours suggested here, or change them to suit your child's room.

MATERIALS

Two 76 x 15cm (30 x 6in) lengths of 2cm (¾in) thick blockboard

Electric drill and a 1.2cm (½in) spade bit

Medium grade sandpaper

Acrylic paint

Shallow dish

Paintbrush

Soft cotton rag

Two 1.8m (2yd) lengths of 1.2cm (½in) diameter blue polyester rope

Remnants of blue and red knitting yarn

10 x 7.5cm (4 x 3in) rectangle of strong card

2.1m (2⅜yd) of pompon braid

Clear craft adhesive

Darning needle or bodkin

Ruler and pencil

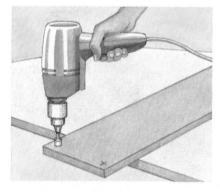

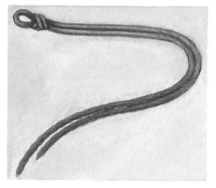

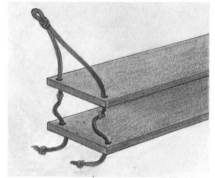

1 PREPARING THE SHELVES
Using the pencil, mark each corner of the blockboard rectangles, 2cm (¾in) in from each edge. Drill a hole with the spade bit right through the wood at each mark. Smooth the cut edges with sandpaper.

2 COLOURING THE WOOD
In the dish, mix a little paint with water to a thin, creamy consistency. Brush the paint on to the wood, then rub it into the grain with the rag. Repeat to achieve a rich colour, then leave it to dry.

3 KNOTTING THE ROPE
Hold the ends of each piece of rope over a flame for a few seconds to seal them. Fold one length of rope in two so that one end is 3cm (1¼in) longer than the other. Tie a knot 3cm (1¼in) from the fold. Repeat to tie a knot in the remaining length of rope.

4 ASSEMBLING THE SHELVES
Mark the rope 42cm (16½in) from the ends. Thread the ends through the holes at one end of one shelf with the longer end at the front. Tie a knot under each mark. Thread the rope through the holes in the other shelf and knot the rope ends. Thread the second rope through the other ends of the shelves and knot it in the same way, with the longer length of rope at the front.

Glue the pompon braid around the sides and front of each shelf.

NOTICEBOARD

This noticeboard is trimmed with brightly coloured felt to match the other furnishings and accessories in the child's bedroom. You can adapt the colours to suit your own scheme.

MATERIALS

62 x 38cm (24½ x 15in) rectangle of 1.2cm (½in) thick softboard

75 x 51cm (29½ x 20in) rectangle of plain cotton fabric

3.6m (4yd) of ricrac braid

Scraps of felt in three or four colours

Nine decorative upholstery nails

Staple gun or drawing pins

Pinking shears (optional)

Mirror clips or heavy duty self-adhesive pads

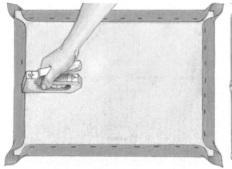

1 COVERING THE BOARD
Lay the board centrally over the wrong side of the fabric. Starting at the centre of one side and working outwards, fix the fabric firmly to the board with staples or drawing pins. Then, pulling the fabric straight and taut, staple or pin the fabric to the opposite side. Repeat to attach the fabric to the remaining sides.

2 SECURING THE CORNERS
At each corner, pull the fabric over the point and secure it with a staple or drawing pin. Fold in the fabric neatly at each side to form a mitre, then secure the folds with staples.

3 ADDING THE BRAID
Arrange the braid in a criss-cross pattern over the front of the board, using the picture as a guide, and stretching the braid taut. Secure it with staples or drawing pins on the wrong side of the board.

4 ATTACHING THE FELT SHAPES
Use pinking shears or scissors to cut your felt scraps into small squares and triangles. Pin the shapes on to the board at the braid cross-over points with the upholstery nails.

▶ Glue colourful beads and paste jewels on to metal containers to make this gleaming desk set. For the pencils, use a craft knife to score two rings near the end of each pencil. Scrape between the rings, then cover this section with embroidery cotton, finishing the ends of the cotton with beads and pompons.

LINED CURTAINS AND ZIGZAG PELMET

Make these easy lined curtains from your boldest patterned fabric and add a pelmet in a coordinating design.

The curtains are made with the lining the same size as the main fabric – this means they're very easy to stitch, and it allows you to make a feature of the lining by looping the curtains back on either side of the window so that it's displayed. Just stitch a curtain ring to each leading edge of the curtain, about two-thirds of the way down, and slip them on to hooks on the wall halfway down the window.

The pelmet adds a classy designer detail. Its lower edge follows the shape of the pattern on the fabric so it's easy to cut out and stitch. If you want to copy this idea on a fabric which doesn't have a suitable pattern, create your own design on paper and use this as a template.

MATERIALS

Two coordinating patterned fabrics

Plain fabric for the lining

Matching sewing thread

Standard curtain tape the width of each finished curtain plus 2cm (¾in)

Double-sided, self-adhesive pelmet stiffener to fit around the front and sides of the pelmet shelf

Standard curtain hooks

Sew-and-stitch touch-and-close fastening to fit around the front and sides of the pelmet shelf

MAKING THE CURTAINS

1 MEASURING UP
Measure the window and decide on the finished length of the curtains. Add 5cm (2in) to the length. To calculate the width, multiply the track by 1½. The fabric width for each curtain should be half this width plus 2cm (¾in); join two lengths of fabric if necessary. Cut out the lining the same size.

> *Tip*
> **SOFT TOUCH**
> If you want a soft pelmet, use craft-weight interfacing fused to mediumweight iron-on interfacing instead of the pelmet interfacing. Cut it the same size as the curtain fabric and sew it in. Trim the seam allowances to reduce bulk.

PAPER FLOWERS

These fantasy paper flowers add a bold decorative detail. They are made from paper ribbon, wire and pipe cleaners.

MATERIALS

For each flower:

Paper ribbon in two colours for the petals, and green for the leaves

Two giant yellow pipe cleaners

1m (1yd) green, paper-covered wire

1.3m (1½yd) of florists' wire

Clear craft adhesive and scissors

leaf template

leaf template

1 CUTTING THE RIBBON
Untwist 60cm (24in) of ribbon for the outer petals and cut it in half. Repeat with the green ribbon. Cut four 32cm (13in) lengths of florists' wire.

petal template

petal template

2 ADDING THE WIRE
Fold each piece of ribbon in half lengthways, then unfold it and spread adhesive on the inside. Lay the wire inside, centred between the fold and the edge. Press the two halves of the paper together, enclosing the wire.

3 CUTTING THE PETALS
For the outer petals, fold the wired ribbon widthways. Trace on the petal pattern, with the straight edge on the fold and the wire in the centre. Cut out the petals.

For the inner petals, cut 15cm (6in) of paper ribbon, smooth it out, then fold it in half lengthways. Cut into it at 5mm (¼in) intervals, leaving 2cm (¾in) uncut at the folded edge. Unfold the petals.

4 ASSEMBLING THE FLOWERS
Unfold the outer petals and lay one over the other. Lay the inner petals on top. Twist both ends of the pipe cleaners around a pencil to make spirals, and lay these on top. Cut 1m (1yd) of paper-covered wire and twist the centre of it around all the layers. Mould the orange petals into a flower shape, twist the wire around the base of the flower, and then round itself to make a stem. Trim the ends.

5 ADDING THE LEAVES
Trace the leaf pattern twice on to the wired green ribbon with the wire running down the centre, and cut it out along the marked lines. Spread adhesive over the base of one leaf for 5cm (2in) and wrap it tightly around the flower stem 18cm (7in) below the flower. Hold the leaf in place until the glue sets, then glue on the other leaf 5cm (2in) further down the stem. Shape the petals and leaves outwards.

ACKNOWLEDGEMENTS

Photographs:
5-16 EM/Martin Chaffer,
17(t,br) IPC Magazines/Robert Harding
    Syndication (bl) EM/John Suett,
18-20 EM/John Suett,
21 IPC Magazines/Robert Harding
    Syndication,
22-24 EM/John Suett,
25-36 EM/Martin Chaffer,
37-48 EM/Steve Tanner,
49-54 EM/Martin Chaffer,
55-61 EM/Adrian Taylor,
62-68(t) EM/Steve Tanner, (b)
    EM/Adrian Taylor,
69 EM/Steve Tanner,
70 EM/Adrian Taylor,
71(t,bl) Ariadne,
71(br) EM/Adrian Taylor,
73,74,75,77 Ariadne,
78 EM/Adrian Taylor,
79(t,bl,bcl,br) Ariadne (bcr)
    EM/Adrian Taylor,
81-83 Ariadne,

85,86 EM/Adrian Taylor,
87 Ariadne,
90 EM/Adrian Taylor,
91-97(tl) Ariadne,
97(c) EM/Simon Page-Ritchie,
98-106 Ariadne,
107-118 EM/Martin Chaffer,
119,120(t) Worldwide Syndication,
121 EM/Simon Page-Ritchie,
122(t) EM/Steve Tanner (b) EM/Simon
    Page-Ritchie,
123-126(t) EM/Simon Page-Ritchie,
126(b) EM/Adrian Taylor,
127-138 EM/Martin Chaffer,
139(t) Ariadne (b) EM/Simon
    Page-Ritchie, 140 Ariadne,
141-146 EM/Simon Page-Ritchie,
147(t) Sheridan Fabrics (b) EM/Adrian
    Taylor,
148-154 EM/Adrian Taylor,
155(c) IPC Magazines/Robert Harding
    Syndication (b) EM/Simon
    Page-Ritchie,

156 IPC Magazines/Robert Harding
    Syndication,
156-157 EM/Simon Page-Ritchie,
158, 159 IPC Magazines/Robert
    Harding Syndication,
160 EM/Simon Page-Ritchie,
161-163 IPC Magazines/Robert
    Harding Syndication,
164 EM/Simon Page-Ritchie,
165 EM/Adrian Taylor, 166 EM/Simon
    Page-Ritchie,
167(l) Ariadne, (r) EM/Adrian Taylor,
168,169(t) Ariadne,
169(b) EM/Adrian Taylor,
171-173 EM/Adrian Taylor,
174 Ariadne,
175-178 EM/Adrian Taylor,
179-190 EM/Martin Chaffer.

Illustrations:
Coral Mula